The
Cat Lover's
Devotional

M. R. Wells
Connie Fleishauer
Dottie P. Adams

HARVEST HOUSE PUBLISHERS

EUGENE, OREGON

Published in association with the literary agency of Mark Sweeney & Associates, Bonita Springs, FL 34135.

Cover by Left Coast Design, Portland, Oregon

Cover photo © iStockphoto / bigworld

The information shared by the authors is from their personal experience and should not be considered professional advice. Readers should consult their own cat care professionals regarding issues related to the health, safety, grooming, and training of their pets.

THE CAT LOVER'S DEVOTIONAL
Copyright © 2011 by M.R. Wells, Connie Fleishauer, and Dottie P. Adams
Published by Harvest House Publishers
Eugene, Oregon 97402
www.harvesthousepublishers.com

Library of Congress Cataloging-in-Publication Data
Wells, M. R. (Marion R.), 1948-
The cat lover's devotional / M.R. Wells, Connie Fleishauer, and Dottie Adams.
   p. cm.
ISBN 978-0-7369-2881-6 (pbk.)
ISBN 978-0-7369-4153-2 (eBook)
1. Cat owners—Prayers and devotions. 2. Cats—Religious aspects—Christianity. I. Fleishauer, Connie. II. Adams, Dottie P., 1944- III. Title.
BV4596.A54W44 2011
242—dc22

                                                           2010049771

Printed in the United States of America

11 12 13 14 15 16 17 18 / VP-NI / 10 9 8 7 6 5 4 3 2 1

To all those who help "purr-fect" us in love:

*Our beloved families and friends,
our treasured kitties, and our infinitely
patient, caring, and forgiving God.*

We write books because You write on our hearts.

Purr-sonal Thanks

Though there are times when we have been catlike and crawled off by ourselves to write, we never could have done this book alone. Thanks to all who let us share their stories on these pages. Thanks to all who lifted us up in prayer. Thanks to Mark and Janet Sweeney, our agents and friends, who help our book dreams come true. Special thanks to Nicole Overbey, DVM, the marvelous vet who took time to "vet" our book and share her feedback with us. And heartfelt thanks to our awesome team at Harvest House Publishers. You are simply the *best*!

Most of all, eternal thanks and praise to our marvelous, matchless Creator God—who made cats for us and "purr-fects" us in love for Himself.

Contents

Part I
Nestling in God's Arms

Part II
Climbing up God's Path

Part III
Basking in God's Comfort

Part IV
Lapping up God's Wisdom

Part V
Hiding in God's Protection

Foreword
How Cats Help "Purr-fect" Us

Some months ago a friend shared a story about an encounter with a cat that I will never forget. She'd never seen the starving stray before, but she went to get it a bowl of milk. When she returned, the tiny cat was attempting to nurse on itself. God whispered to my friend's heart, "That's what you do when you try to meet your own needs all by yourself instead of coming to Me."

God intends us to be in relationship. That's where love happens. That's where our character grows. That's the canvas on which He lovingly places each of us to "purr-fect" us into His one-of-a-kind masterpiece for eternity. Part of that canvas involves our kitties—for those of us who love them. God can use them to show us more about ourselves, each other, and Him—if we have eyes to see.

Like us, cats can be capricious. Like us, they can have a strong independent streak. Like us, they need their master...at times more than they know. And just as we long to hold, guide, comfort, and protect our beloved kitties and help them grow and thrive, God longs to do this for us.

Being "purr-fected" in love is a journey. We have shared part of ours on these pages. We have shared how God uses the kitties we know and love to work in us for our good and His glory. We pray He will use their tales and ours to enrich your life too, and help you know Him better.

Meet the Kitties

 **BARNEY WELLS** had a deep chocolate coat and beautiful green eyes. Of all my cats, he was the biggest talker. He meowed for his due in life and for release, when it was time.

BO WELLS is a handsome flame point Ragdoll I call my giant plush toy. He loves his food, his water bowl, and rubbing against his mommy's feet. He had to slay some "giants" to join my family, but now he thinks he rules the roost.

 **GABRIEL WELLS** was once and always an alley cat. At nine years of age my black-and-white buddy vanished from my life—but not from my heart.

MISTY WELLS was a beautiful blue point Birman. She was small in stature but had a huge spirit. She demanded respect from the larger cats and much larger humans in her life, even in her twilight years.

MUFFIN WELLS is a gorgeous seal point Ragdoll who looks and acts like a princess with paws. She used to chase the small round shadow of my watch face as if it were real. It wasn't, but my love for her is, and she likes nothing better than to cuddle with her mama.

KITTY FLEISHAUER was a beautiful black cat with white on her tail and paws. She mothered not only her own kittens, but others that came to our farm. She also tried to protect her people, following our  family all over our property up to her own personal boundary lines. This kitty truly held each of our hearts.

MIDNIGHT ADAMS can go in one split second from purring in ecstasy to pouncing on the hand that motivated the purrs. When this "black beauty" patrols her domain, she reminds us of a panther on the prowl.

MOOCH ADAMS is a gorgeous gray tabby with white highlights on his paws, face, and chest. He plays with toys more than any other cat we've had and is quite a catcher. He loves hanging out with  us and whenever he sees us, he runs to greet us—meowing all the way.

Part I

Nestling in God's Arms

🐾 MIDNIGHT 🐾

Midnight's Not-So-Rapid Transit
Relationships Take Time

*We always have time enough, if
we will but use it aright.*

JOHANN WOLFGANG VON GOETHE

I love sitting at the dining room table on spring mornings, watching the stark darkness turn into a misty dawn as the birds sing to announce the new day. It's a great time to be alone with the Lord. The house is quiet because I'm the only "early bird" up besides the real ones chirping outside.

As I sat praying one particular morning I heard a loud thump on the window behind me. It was Midnight, asking to come in for breakfast. She always bangs her head against the windowpane to get my attention. Then she rubs her nose against the window frame and meows softly, knowing I will come outside to fetch her. I call this her "rapid transit," even though she could come in much more quickly through the cat door. But it's not the quickness she desires—it's the contact.

As Midnight softly meowed and rubbed that morning I pulled on a jacket and headed outdoors to perform the rite we both love. I cozy up to the air conditioner, which is exactly the height of my shoulders. She steps from the machine to my shoulder as I guide her. She drapes herself around me with her front paws on my left shoulder, her belly nestling the back of my neck, and her back paws hanging down over my right shoulder. As her face presses against me, she purrs into my left ear. I understand that this is her ride to her food bowl—but it's so much more. Not only do I get a smell of the morning air, I have precious moments of special closeness with my "living fur shawl." It's a joy to have this relationship with one of God's little four-foots—a joy I treasure!

Like my cat, my youngest grandchild also loves to cuddle. He and his brother and their parents live with us right now. I often spend part of the morning upstairs working on lectures for the Bible study class I teach. Eli and Jayden are awake by the time I come downstairs. Jayden (age two and a half) is content to smile, call to me, and continue his play. But Eli (18 months) wants more. He rushes over to me, crying "Maw-Maw!" Then he tugs at my clothes till I pick him up so he can snuggle. As soon as he's in my arms, he lays his head tightly against me, his ear pressed against my chest. He stays that way for what is a long time for a toddler. It's a joy to have this special time with him, and I treasure it too!

I also treasure the special relationship time I spend with God. Most mornings I go to Him in prayer, even if it's just to ask His blessing on my family. I spend a few moments reading the Bible, even if it's just one verse to connect my mind to Him. I call this "having coffee with Jesus."

I get my coffee and intentionally ask Jesus to sit with me as if He were here in the flesh. I picture Him sitting right across the table. I talk about the previous day or the day to come. I weep with Him over hardships I'm facing or the suffering of others. I laugh and rejoice with Him over answered prayer. I share my needs and thank Him for being my friend. Sometimes I imagine Him smiling back at me, and other times I believe He brings a verse of Scripture into my mind to correct me or give me hope or courage.

Building close relationships takes time. It must be intentional. It can't only happen when it's convenient. Jesus lived this out when He walked the earth. He called each of His disciples and poured His life into them for three years. And He always took time to pray and be with His Father in heaven.

Midnight intentionally bumps the window to begin our special time together. I intentionally respond, even if she's interrupting something pressing. When Eli wants to snuggle, I take time to enjoy his toddler love, even if I'm in a hurry. I have coffee with Jesus in the same way. Whether it's convenient or not, I take the necessary time not just to go through my prayers, but to be with my Lord. I believe He delights to hear me purring in His ear as I start the day with Him!

In the morning, LORD, you hear my voice; in the morning I lay my requests before you and wait expectantly (Psalm 5:3).

Consider This:

Do you set aside time to be with God each day? If so, how does it enhance your relationship? If not, would you be willing to try?

Perry's Good Shepherd

Be a Shepherd for God

The King of love my Shepherd is,
Whose goodness faileth never;
I nothing lack if I am His,
And He is mine forever.

Henry W. Baker

Perry is a very special kitty, the first to live indoors with my in-laws, Harold and Doris. They got him from relatives who could no longer keep him. He is totally enjoying his new life as he chooses where to sleep and whose lap to jump on for some pampering. This gorgeous fluffy orange cat with bright peridot eyes knows just what he wants and how to get it. He loves Harold and Doris, but like all ornery kids he knows how to work them.

On one particular evening when I'd been visiting with them, Perry decided to be a bit more playful than anyone desired. When we walked out the back door, Perry slipped out behind us and followed. He darted under my car to hide. I saw him first and began to call him, but there was no way he was going to obey me. This was playtime. He raced to the back of the vehicle and sprinted down the long driveway.

Harold and Doris live in the country, but their home is near a popular road where cars drive fast. Perry could have been in great danger. He would have had little chance of survival on this road in the dark of night. Fortunately, his faithful master took care of him. As I started to go after the truant, Harold stopped me. He said, "Cover me with the flashlight and I'll go get him."

Although Perry was ornery, perhaps this cat had some "horse sense." He got close to the road but turned aside. He darted into the pasture at the east end of the farm. Perry slunk down in the high grass while Harold, age 82, tried to sneak up on the mischievous feline in his stocking feet in the dark. I felt bad that Harold would not let me join him in the pursuit, but this was his cat, his "child," his responsibility. He was Perry's "good shepherd," and he was acting as any good shepherd would. Giving up or giving in was never an option.

Finally, Perry seemed to realize that Harold was in charge (or he chose to let Harold think he was). Perry hunkered down and let his human grab him. I could tell that even though Harold was tired and his stocking feet were muddy, he was pleased to have Perry back safely in his arms.

Harold probably just thought of this as another one of many chases he had with Perry. But to me, it was more. It was a reenactment of the Parable of the Lost Sheep. In Matthew 18:12-14, Jesus talks about the shepherd who left the rest of his flock to search for the one little lost sheep that had wandered off.

Many years ago, I was just such a lost sheep. Just before entering high school, I had been making some very poor choices. I had accepted Jesus as my personal Savior when I was six years old, and I had gone to church all my life. But at this time, I decided to explore my small world in ways I didn't need to. I had chosen to be with some "friends" who weren't true friends, and we had done some things we needed to confess.

My older brother talked to me about what I was doing. He asked if I really wanted to go to high school with that baggage. He stayed with me until I prayed and promised that I would try to obey God and behave like His child. Darrell was my shepherd at that point, and many other times through my teenage years. When I was lost, he went looking for me till he found me. He'd bring me home and nurture me the way a brother or a shepherd would.

The story of the lost sheep had great meaning to me as I was growing up. I loved thinking about the caring shepherd picking up the scared, tired little lamb in his strong arms and carrying it home. I still take comfort in this parable today. It is a way of telling us that we will never be left alone. No matter what our age, if we choose to run off by ourselves, like Perry did that night, our Good Shepherd will always go after us and bring us home in His loving arms, if we allow Him to.

Suppose one of you has a hundred sheep and loses one of them. Doesn't he leave the ninety-nine in the open country and go after the lost sheep until he finds it? And when he finds it, he joyfully puts it on his shoulders and goes home. Then he calls his friends and neighbors together and says, "Rejoice with me; I have found my lost sheep." I tell you that in the same way there will be more rejoicing in heaven over one sinner who repents than over ninety-nine righteous persons who do not need to repent (Luke 15:4-7).

Consider This:

Have you ever strayed from God? What lured you away? How did your Good Shepherd pursue you? Did you let Him carry you home? If not, would you like to do that right now? Is there someone God might want you to shepherd for Him?

Undying Love
Be "Otherly"

*True happiness is found in unselfish Love, a Love
which increases in proportion as it is shared.*

THOMAS MERTON

Tigret was my dear friend Patty's treasured four-footed kitty soul mate for 17 wonderful years. He was her first real pet and best buddy. They lived together in New York, and when Patty moved to California, Tigret made the cross-country journey with her.

When Patty watched TV, Tigret would curl up beside her. He slept on her bed at night. When she gave parties, he sat on his very own chair. But he was more than a faithful companion. Patty once heard someone say that God gives us each a pet to teach us something special. She feels Tigret was given to her to teach her to be "otherly"—to love others and God with an unselfish love.

Tigret knew Patty's moods. He sensed when she was sad or happy. He would put his paw on her lap or hand in a gesture of kitty comfort. He also seemed to know when she was sick—sometimes even before she did. He would stay close by his beloved human until he sensed she was better.

Tigret's ultimate expression of unselfish love was to care for Patty even when he was dying. He was 17 and had developed kidney problems. He couldn't drink enough water to stay healthy, and giving him fluids subcutaneously didn't work well. He would yelp when the needle was inserted. Patty decided not to force this on him. Tigret got sicker and sicker until it took all his strength just to go upstairs. Clearly Tigret's time on this earth was ending. Patty made him as comfortable as she could…even as her own heart was breaking.

One day, as Patty tended Tigret in tears, he reached out his paw and placed it on her arm. It was as if he was saying, "You'll be okay." When Tigret died, Patty wasn't with him. She believes he knew it would be easier for her that way.

Someone else in Patty's life also tried to care for her while dying. Patty's mother passed away just one month after Tigret. She had battled cancer before—but no one knew it had come back.

Patty's mom was a pediatric cardiologist. In her later years she semi-retired from private practice and became involved in teaching and mentoring medical interns and residents. She kept this up even when the cancer returned, and Patty would not have realized that something was wrong except for God's intervention.

It was a Sunday after church, and Patty had gone up front for prayer on a completely unrelated matter. The gentleman who prayed with her asked Patty how her mother was. "As far as I know, okay," Patty answered. The man suggested Patty ask her mom about her health. When Patty did, her mom admitted her cancer had come back.

Just like Tigret, Patty's mom was concerned for the needs of others, even as her own health was failing. She tried to keep teaching. She talked to Patty about taking care of her dad. When Patty finally persuaded her to go to the doctor, he said she had six to nine months to live. They could try chemotherapy, but there was no guarantee.

Patty's mom took her first dose of chemo—and passed away a week later.

Patty recalls a moment in her mother's hospital room. Her mom was on a ventilator. Patty saw two angels in a corner by the bed. Patty knew her mom loved Jesus and would go to be with Him. She died soon after. That experience feels to Patty like a special gift from God.

Our loving Lord Jesus was also "otherly" when it was time for Him to die. As His betrayal and crucifixion approached, His focus was to teach and prepare His disciples. In John 16:5-7, He told them, "Now I am going to him who sent me. None of you asks me, 'Where are you going?' Rather, you are filled with grief because I have said these things. But very truly I tell you, it is for your good that I am going away. Unless I go away, the Advocate will not come to you; but if I go, I will send him to you." Even as He hung on the cross, Jesus asked His disciple John to care for His mother.

But Jesus' sacrificial love went far deeper. He willingly took upon Himself the penalty for our sins. By doing so, He conquered sin and death so that all who put their trust in Him could enjoy eternal life. Patty has given her life to her Savior, and she knows that when she leaves this earth she will go to her loving Lord, who will wipe away all her tears, including the ones she shed for Tigret and her mother. And she'll be reunited with her mom again.

Being "otherly" isn't something that starts when we are dying. It's a way of life. It's what Jesus calls us to do. If you live and love with an "otherly" focus, as Tigret and Patty's mom did, you will show that you are Jesus' disciple!

This is love: not that we loved God, but that he loved us and sent his Son as an atoning sacrifice for our sins. Dear friends, since God so loved us, we also ought to love one another (1 John 4:10-11).

Consider This:

Is there someone in your life who loves you unselfishly? How do they do that and how does it make you feel? How could you focus more on others and be more sensitive to their needs? What could you do to show them "otherly" love?

For the Love of a Cat
Love Lets Go

*We cannot do great things on this Earth,
only small things with great love.*

MOTHER TERESA

Andrea's heart broke the first time she saw the gorgeous longhaired gray-tone tortoiseshell cat. Maybe it was the kitty's matted fur and dirty appearance; maybe it was the fact that this cat had to live in a cage—but Andrea knew she had to help. When she heard the cat's long, soft meow, it was love at first sound. After several visits, Andrea and her husband, our son Sam, brought the kitty home. They named her Jazz.

Jazz had a strong, vibrant personality. Her new surroundings didn't intimidate her in the least. Laska, their larger-than-normal border collie, didn't faze her. Neither did three lively children, all under the age of six. When the children dragged her around, she went limp and let them. She seemed completely at ease when Laska watched from a nose-length as she drank his water. He didn't scare her even one little bit! Pets and humans all seemed to sense that this was a match made in heaven.

Jazz's new home was in a fairly safe neighborhood, so Sam put in a little cat door. Jazz loved the freedom to come and go. Though she was independent, at times she craved love from her humans and was quite insistent in asking for it. They, of course, were delighted to oblige. When I first met Jazz, she struck me as a cat whose home and life were wonderfully suited to her. She even visited the neighbors when the kids went out to play. She didn't just own her own home and family, she owned the entire block! This place was hers and she was content.

Sam and Andrea thought this match would last for Jazz's entire lifetime. That was not to be. Due to financial difficulties, Sam had to move his family out of the city and into a less expensive, more rural area. Their new neighborhood held great dangers for little cats. They couldn't let her out anymore. But Jazz was used to going outside whenever she desired. One evening, she bolted through the door before Andrea could even think about stopping her. Andrea called her and searched for her but couldn't find her. One new neighbor feared an owl or coyote had carried her away. Andrea spent a sleepless night of worry. But then, as if by magic, Jazz strolled into the house the next morning. It was then that Andrea made a very difficult and selfless decision for her little cat.

A dear friend and neighbor of hers on the old street adored Jazz too—so much so that she'd said she wished the little cat belonged to her. Andrea called this friend, Nicole, and told her what had happened. She asked Nicole to adopt Jazz. Nicole was delighted. Andrea took Jazz to her new home that very afternoon. It was extremely hard for Andrea and she still misses her beloved kitty, but she knows this was the best thing for her pet. Jazz is back on the block she loves, can go outdoors safely again, and is with a new family who will care for and cherish her also.

Jazz is completely happy in her new home. She already knew Nicole, her husband, and their two children. Their two dogs don't intimidate her either. She's been with them several months now, and if you didn't know any different, you'd think Jazz had lived there forever. She adores her new life and family. And Andrea takes comfort in knowing that her beloved kitty is safe and happy.

Sam's biological mother made a similar call in his life before he was born. She was an unwed mother who decided her child would fare better in this life if he were given up for adoption. She wanted him to be raised in a settled home with both a mom and a dad who would love and provide for him. The adoption agency made sure her wishes for this child were fulfilled, and that's why my husband and I were selected. Her stipulations were that he be the firstborn of the family, be raised in a Protestant home, and have parents who would encourage him to go to college. It had to be a wrenching decision to let him go, but her love and concern for his well-being gave her the strength. Just as Andrea was able to give Jazz up for her own good, so Sam's biological mother gave him up for his best.

Sam is the oldest of our three children. He is currently working on his doctorate in theology. He is a wonderful man: brilliant, respectable, faithful, and filled with integrity. If his biological mother could see him now, she would know she made the right choice. My husband and I have been completely blessed by raising Sam, and we are humbled and honored to have him as our son. It was an amazing opportunity to bring a baby into our home that way. We know it was a match made in heaven.

The first adoption mentioned in the Bible was also a match made in heaven. At the time, the Israelites were slaves in Egypt. Things had gotten progressively worse and they were crying out to God for rescue. Pharaoh had commanded that all male Hebrew babies be killed at birth. But a Levite woman named Jochebed was desperate to save her son (Exodus 2). She hid the baby for three months. When concealing him became impossible, she did the hardest thing ever—she let him go. She fashioned a little papyrus basket into a boat by coating it with tar and pitch. She placed it along the bank of the Nile with her child inside, and walked away. She left the boy's older sister to watch at a distance and tell her what happened. Perhaps she knew Pharaoh's daughter bathed there and was hoping that she or a servant would rescue the child.

And that's exactly what happened. Pharaoh's daughter spied the basket and sent a slave to retrieve it. She found the baby inside and took pity on him. She realized this was a Hebrew child. At that moment Moses' sister approached and offered to get a nurse for him from among the Hebrew women. The girl brought Jochebed, and Pharaoh's daughter paid her to take and nurse her own child till he was weaned. Jochebed then returned the boy to the Egyptian princess, who adopted him as her own son.

Jochebed gave up her son out of love—first to the river, and then to

Pharaoh's daughter. She let him go so he could have life. If you don't know the rest of the story, this boy was Moses, who later became God's chosen deliverer of Israel. It was Moses who, at God's command, instituted the first Passover and led his people out of Egypt and slavery. Jochebed had no idea what her son's future might hold. She just wanted to see to it that he had life. Selfless love enabled her to let him go—and God granted her heart's deepest longing and then multiplied the blessing.

Selfless love lets go. It places the loved one's welfare above our own. That's why Andrea gave Jazz to Nicole. That's why Sam's biological mom released him to us. That's why Jochebed put her child in a basket on the Nile. And that's why God the Father sent His Son Jesus to die for us. When we love in this way, we love God's way. This pleases Him and releases His blessings.

[Love] always protects, always trusts, always hopes, always perseveres. Love never fails (1 Corinthians 13:7-8).

Consider This:

Have you ever had to give up a child or pet to better their life? Have you been able to put your loved one in God's hands? If so, how did that help? In what other ways might you show selfless love to others?

Lovin' Troubles
Love Turns Trouble into Blessing

Life is mostly froth and bubble,
Two things stand like stone,
Kindness in another's trouble,
Courage in your own.

ADAM LINDSAY GORDON

Troubles was trouble in the beginning, but became no trouble at all. And therein hangs a cat tail…um, tale.

Troubles is part Siamese with raccoon markings on her tail. She wasn't always looking for trouble—it just came easily to her. When she was a little kitten she knocked down the Christmas tree, freeing it from all the ornaments and other collected decorations. She stopped climbing trees after that—until one day when she was six months old. She got chased by some dogs and scurried up a tree in her front yard so fast and high that some tree trimmers had to come and help her down.

These escapades earned Troubles her name. But her master, my friend Pat, adores her. I have never met anyone who loves their cat more. Pat is not married and travels all over the country in her van with only Troubles as her companion. Troubles has her own carrier to ride in and a special pillow for a bed. Pat told me Troubles' favorite time is at night, when they can sleep quietly without the van moving, or when the little cat can curl up on Pat's lap to be petted and have all her attention.

Pat is one of my swimming friends. We meet three times a week and trade life stories while we exercise in the pool. Pat tells us all about what's happening with Troubles. Pat's "baby" is now a senior cat battling bone cancer. But she just celebrated her 16th birthday with three helpings of tuna and a houseful of people singing "Happy Birthday" to her.

Now that Troubles has health trouble, Pat is doing everything she can for her feline companion. I am amazed at the trouble she'll take for this cat. I had farm cats most of my life, and as much as we loved them, we could never afford to spend a lot of money on them. Pat has the funds and gladly shares them with Troubles to keep her comfortable. She drives her cat to a veterinary specialty hospital in Los Angeles, over 100 miles away. They give Troubles special testing and treatment for her condition. Just recently, Pat also got Troubles some dental work so she could enjoy her food.

It hurts Pat to know that Troubles probably doesn't have a lot of time left on earth. But she continues to put Troubles' needs ahead of her own. Pat loves Troubles, so to her, taking special care of her very special kitty is really no trouble at all.

Like Pat's cat, I recently found trouble without looking for it. Five months ago, I fell at the community theater. It ended up being a huge problem. I had to be taken to the hospital in an ambulance—but that was just the beginning. I developed a huge hematoma—a swollen area filled with blood from internal bleeding—in my right leg. I couldn't use that leg, so I needed a wheelchair. I couldn't get around much without help and wound up spending a lot of time at home.

My oldest daughter, Christy, and her soon-to-be husband, Steve, helped a great deal by taking me to various medical appointments. One day, Steve pushed me several blocks from the doctor's office to the X-ray technician. We had been told it was just a short way, but we were given the wrong directions. It took much longer than we thought, and I was in a great deal of pain. But through it all, Steve was gentle and sweet, and Christy went back to get our car so I wouldn't have another wheelchair ride to where it had been parked. I felt terrible for taking up so much of their time. But to Steve it was no trouble at all. He just said, "What better way to spend time than with future family?"

When Jesus walked this earth, He took the trouble to care about lots of people others would have called "trouble." This motley group included tax collectors, a woman taken in adultery, lepers, and a whole Samaritan village. Jesus even went to the cross and died for our sins so His great trouble could heal our troubles forever. As the prophet Isaiah wrote, "He was pierced for our transgressions, he was crushed for our iniquities; the punishment that brought us peace was on him, and by his wounds we are healed" (Isaiah 53:5).

Love not only makes trouble no trouble, it turns it into blessing. It surely did for Pat and her cat, and for Steve and me. Ask God to fill you with His love so you can bless those in trouble and be blessed in return.

In this world you will have trouble. But take heart! I have overcome the world (John 16:33).

Consider This:

Do you know someone you try to avoid because he or she is "trouble"? What do you fear might happen if you reached out? Would you be willing for God to change this? Would you pray for this person right now, and ask God to fill you with His love?

Freeing Tigger
Let God's Love Liberate You

*In essentials, unity; in nonessentials,
liberty; in all things, charity.*

SAINT AUGUSTINE

When my friend Stephanie was growing up in Michigan, her family often took in abandoned pets. Due to the extremes of weather and lack of food, animals who were left to fend for themselves often couldn't make it. Stephanie's family reached out to these four-footed orphans by feeding them and providing shelter. That's how Stephanie met a beautiful gray tabby cat named Tigger.

When Stephanie first saw Tigger, he refused to come to her. Stephanie knew he had been abandoned because he wore a flea collar. He had such a sweet face that she wanted to pick him up and love him. But he responded to her overtures by bolting off her porch instead.

Every time Stephanie approached him, Tigger would run and hide. Maybe that's why it took several days for her to notice that Tigger had one paw hooked into his flea collar. Somehow he had put his paw through the collar—perhaps in an effort to get it off—but his paw got stuck. The collar was stretched under his front leg and around his neck.

Maybe that was why he wouldn't let anyone get near him. He only came around for the food they left out so he wouldn't starve.

Tigger was suffering from that collar, but he probably didn't understand what was wrong. Stephanie was determined to cut it off. The next time he came for food she grabbed him—despite the risk of getting bitten or scratched. Tigger fought her, hissing and growling, but she somehow managed to cut the collar away.

Tigger fled again, but he seemed to have understood her kindness. The very next time he came for food, he lingered a bit, allowing Stephanie to touch him. This began a love relationship between them. Tigger started to come around even when it wasn't time to eat. He watched for Stephanie to walk outside, and when she did, he ran over to her, rubbing her legs as she petted him. Soon he began to purr before she even touched him. Tigger became her special cat. Whenever she came outdoors, he hung out with her. If she was sitting on the porch, he curled up in her lap and lay there contentedly until she got up. Tigger became part of the family and Stephanie's all-time favorite kitty, all because she cut away the collar that was blocking their relationship.

Tigger's collar was originally meant to help him. It was supposed to keep him free of fleas. But because he got tangled in it, the collar had a very different effect. We humans also sometimes get hung up in "collars" that, though meant for good, wind up hindering our relationships with each other and God.

My dear friend Peggy needed to have such a "collar" cut away. She was raised in a solid, Bible-believing church from the time she was a baby. She knew more Bible verses as a teen than most of us know in a lifetime. But the knowledge she had didn't help her love others. Her Bible knowledge, like Tigger's collar, was meant to help her, but she got tangled in it and it had the opposite result. She became prideful, thinking her church alone had the complete truth. When she started getting to know another believer and found out that her new friend had a different view than she did on some aspect of her faith, she pulled back. Her collar hindered her from having close relationships. Instead of helping her to love others, her Scripture knowledge became a barrier between them. She needed someone to get her paw out of that collar.

Peggy's loving heavenly Father did just that. He cut her collar and freed her to become one of the most loving women I know. He did it by getting her involved in an interdenominational Bible study class. There she learned that others could have a strong faith in Jesus like hers, yet not see eye-to-eye with her on things that didn't involve salvation. She came to understand that Christians can have different beliefs on many issues as long as they agree on the gospel: that Jesus was the incarnation of God in human flesh, lived a sinless life, was crucified, was buried, and rose again on the third day—then ascended to heaven where He now sits at the right hand of the Father. She realized that her knowledge had caused her to judge others rather than truly loving them as God desired.

By cutting away her collar of pride through her new friends, God freed Peggy to be all He wanted her to be. He called Peggy to teach a Bible study class in which she used the knowledge she had in the way He intended—to love others. Her heavenly Father's love had freed her from what was holding her back, just as Stephanie's love had freed Tigger.

That was many years ago. I've been privileged to share a friendship with Peggy over several decades. Freed from that collar, she has loved hundreds of people and encouraged them to learn without becoming prideful. She has just retired from teaching that class after 20 years, and I have been honored to watch what God has done in and through her life.

Paul the apostle also had to cut away collars of pride in the early church so God's love could flow freely. He wrote to the Corinthians, "Knowledge puffs up, but love builds up. The man who thinks he knows something does not yet know as he ought to know. But the man who loves God is known by God" (1 Corinthians 8:1-3). Paul understood what Peggy came to realize—that we have limited knowledge and must recognize that God alone knows it all.

Sometimes, like Tigger and Peggy, we don't catch on to what's hindering our love. But God knows what's keeping us from loving Him and others with our whole hearts. If we allow Him to cut away the "collars" that are holding us back, it will free us to walk more closely with Him and with our brothers and sisters in Christ. And in so doing we'll become all He intended—and be blessed.

If I speak in the tongues of men or of angels, but do not have love, I am only a resounding gong or a clanging cymbal. If I have the gift of prophecy and can fathom all mysteries and all knowledge, and if I have a faith that can move mountains, but do not have love, I am nothing (1 Corinthians 13:1-2).

Consider This:

Have you ever felt you couldn't love others because your paw was caught in your collar? Did you understand what was hindering you, or were you confused? Have you allowed God to cut the collar away? If so, what were the results? If not, would you pray and ask Him to do so?

A Cat for All Seasons
Roles Change, but Our Place in God's Heart Doesn't

Do not worry about holding high position;
worry rather about playing your proper role.

CONFUCIUS

Kitty was definitely one of our family's favorite cats. She was with us the longest and consequently gave us the most cat memories. She was a "cat for all seasons" and played various roles in our family during the years we had her.

Kitty started out as an orphan. Our youngest daughter, Karen, had wanted a kitten for some time. We had dropped our older children off at band camp and were with Karen in Atascadero, some distance from our Bakersfield, California, home. We looked in the paper and found an ad from the local animal shelter. When we got there, we learned a lady had brought in a litter of tiny kittens only a few weeks old. A little black one with white on her chest grabbed our hearts. We welcomed Kitty into our family that very day.

We all loved Kitty and took care of her. She was everybody's baby. She lived in the house when she was little and seldom went outside. She was sweet and dependent then. But as she got older she came to like it better outdoors, and grew into a beautiful, independent adult cat.

Kitty not only took care of herself; she was soon caring for babies of her own. She took her new role of mama quite seriously. When she had kittens, she was very cautious with them. She would hide them around the farm in places where they were safe from other animals. One time, she kept her kittens in an old pickup truck, so we named them after old cars we had. Two of those kittens, Chevy and Beamer, now live with our daughter Christy. Kitty must have liked her mothering role, because it seemed she never gave us time to get her spayed. After a litter was weaned she'd leave our farm for a while. When she came back, she was often pregnant again.

In her adult years, Kitty also started watching over her human family. When we were outside, she stayed next to us. If my husband Steve and our son John were working on a vehicle in our farm's shop, Kitty hung out there and followed them around. When we took a walk, Kitty would come with us—but only to the end of the orchard. She would sit waiting until we returned and then join us again for the trip back to the house. She was our resident "guard cat," but only on our property.

Kitty wore many hats in our family over the years. But her place in our hearts always stayed the same. I think our place in hers did too. Everyone always loved Kitty and we knew she loved us!

My sister Bonnie also had changing roles in my life over the years. She was the second-oldest of five children. I was the youngest. She had her firstborn son, Phil, when I was only 11 years old. She lived over a hundred miles away. She would often invite me to come to her home for a couple of weeks at a time to play with her little boy. My big sister didn't have much money, but we always had a wonderful time.

After I was grown and had a family, our relationship shifted a bit. The age difference between us was less important. Bonnie would often come to our home and we would visit. We would laugh about silly things, fight like sisters, and always love each other.

These days Bonnie is the only one of my three sisters who lives in my hometown. We have plenty of time to spend together, and do. Because we are Bonnie and Connie, she likes to jokingly tell people we are twins—and in a way we are. We can sit down for peanut butter ice cream and laugh until we cry. Then we might cry until we laugh. At the end of it all, we hug and go back to our own lives.

Bonnie and I hold different positions in relation to each other than we once did, but our love for one another has stayed constant—and it always will.

God's children also play varying roles in His family. I started singing special music in church when I was four years old. I sang alto in duets and trios with other kids and we had to stand on chairs so people could see us. In high school I helped lead a youth choir and taught Sunday school. I also helped with Vacation Bible School (VBS) and was in student leadership of Youth for Christ. As an adult I've been involved in everything from music and drama to women's ministry, VBS, Sunday school, and church planting. I've been part of a group who prays for the entertainment industry. Of late, I've also been writing devotional books—like this one. But though I've worn many hats, God's love shines down on me equally no matter which one I have on.

Moses was a biblical character who also wore many hats in his life. He was born a Hebrew. He became an orphan floating in a basket on the Nile. He was adopted by Pharaoh's daughter and raised to be a prince. In adulthood, he appointed himself a defender of his Hebrew kin and struck an abusive slave master dead. He had to flee for his life and became a fugitive. Then he was a shepherd in Midian, and a husband and father. Finally, God called Moses to lead his people out of Egypt. At first, he was a reluctant deliverer. His initial reaction was, in effect, "Here I am. Send someone else." Over time, though, Moses became God's willing servant, a mighty prophet, a dynamic leader of the Hebrews, and the writer of the first five books of the Bible. His role in life and in God's family shifted dramatically over his lifetime and God used him in incredible ways. But God loved the tiny baby floating on the Nile just as much as the venerated prophet He gathered to Himself in Moab at 120 years of age.

The roles we play may grow and change us, but who we are is more than that. We knew this about Kitty, and God knows this about us. The special place God has for me in His heart isn't labeled sister, daughter, or mother. It's not labeled writer, singer, or teacher. It's not any more or less high or wide or deep because of what I do for Him. This bottomless, unfathomable, unchanging place of unending love is simply labeled "Connie," and it is mine forever.

And I pray that you, being rooted and established in love, may have power, together with all the Lord's holy people, to grasp how wide and long and high and deep is the love of Christ, and to know this love that surpasses knowledge—that you may be filled to the measure of all the fullness of God (Ephesians 3:17-19).

Consider This:

Does the role people play in your life affect their place in your heart? How could you love them more unconditionally? Do you feel God's love for you is affected by what you do for Him? How does this help or hinder your walk with the Lord?

The Pruning of Cats and People
Bald Will Be Beautiful

Instinct must be thwarted just as one prunes
the branches of a tree so that it will grow better.

HENRI MATISSE

Muffin is a gorgeous seal point Ragdoll kitty with thick, plush fur. When her fur is healthy, it's a beauty to behold. But it's also the type that can get quite matted if it's not kept up. One recent year, both Muffin and I fell down on our grooming job. My cat's fur got thick with tangles. I realized something had to be done, and went to work to "prune" it of its multitude of knots.

Muffin's mats did not give way gently, even with a special grooming tool. She hated having her fur pulled. *I should never have let things get this bad,* I thought. She expressed her displeasure, and fought submitting to my efforts. I kept at it and managed to get all the clumpy mats out in the end…but she lost a lot of fur in the process. I realized to my horror that part of Muffin's back looked all but bald. In the midst of her longer fur, there was a spot where her coat was so sparse it barely covered her skin. Have you ever seen a lawn with a bare patch? That was my poor kitty!

I knew Muffin was better off for having those mats groomed. I knew they had to be gone for her fur to get healthy. But I winced inside every time I looked at her. It seemed her baldness went on for weeks. I started wondering if her new fur would ever grow in. It seemed to be getting slightly longer, but it had a ways to go.

Then, for whatever reason, I stopped noticing Muffin's fur so much. And suddenly one day I saw it was back! She looked lush and plush once more!

Muffin's very visible outward pruning exemplifies the way God works with each of His children. He must prune each of us to stimulate healthy new growth. And, like the de-matting of Muffin, it can prove to be a somewhat painful process…at least in the beginning.

A dear friend called Tammy recently went through just such a pruning period. She'd had a bumpy childhood, and it left a mark. Her parents had divorced. Her living situation had fluctuated. Having a house of her own became a symbol of stability, and it was extremely important to her.

Tammy had come to know the Lord as a young adult. She had a mature, loving Christian husband and wonderful children. But, deep inside, the emotional need for her own home was still very strong. Her husband knew this and longed to fulfill those deep desires, hoping it would have a healing effect.

The young couple bought a home in a small city in the Pacific Northwest. Tammy's husband pastored a church and worked on the side to help make ends meet. He was also in a long-distance Master's program with an overseas seminary. But his deepest dream and sense of calling from God was to teach theology at the college level. He had put that dream on hold and didn't know if it would ever come true.

God knew. He would prune Tammy so He could bless them both.

The economic crisis hit. Work became scarce in their city. Making the mortgage payment was a huge monthly stress. In the midst of the struggle, God began to speak to Tammy's heart. He was pruning away her attachment to a physical house, and showing her that her true home and stability were rooted in her husband and children, not her physical surroundings. With no prodding or prompting from her husband, Tammy went to him and suggested that if he wanted to pursue his teaching dreams, she would be behind him.

God's pruning process had begun. So did His blessing. He opened up an opportunity for Tammy's husband to pursue a Ph.D. God provided financial support and even an unexpected scholarship. But it meant the young family had to leave their house, their city, and even their country and go to study abroad.

It wasn't easy for Tammy, but she knew God was in it. Even as she broke down in tears, she pushed forward. She and her husband could both see that this was what God wanted for them, and she was willing to go through the "bald" phase of her pruning so they could both become "lush and plush" in their service to God. As I write this, they are getting settled in a new country and town and he will soon begin work on his doctoral degree. Even as they fight through the homesickness, they are excited to see how God will work.

Many centuries ago, God pruned an Old Testament prophet named Jonah. He'd told Jonah to preach repentance to the city of Nineveh. But Jonah didn't want these pagans to escape God's wrath—so he fled. God arranged for Jonah to get swallowed by a "great fish." Jonah called out to God in his distress, got spat out by the fish, and went on to obey his prophetic call. Even then, Jonah's heart attitude had a few mats and tangles left, and God graciously pruned those out too so Jonah could better understand God's compassion (Jonah 4).

Muffin the cat had no idea why I was working on her tangled fur. She didn't know I was doing it for her good. And, truth be told, I was far from perfect in my method and timing. God is a perfect parent and gardener. He knows just when to take His divine pruning shears to our lives. He knows just what and how much to remove to stimulate healthy growth in Him. Will you submit to God's loving pruning and trust Him through the "bald" times of life, knowing they will result in rich blessing and fruit for His kingdom?

I am the true vine, and my Father is the gardener. He cuts off every branch in me that bears no fruit, while every branch that does bear fruit he prunes so that it will be even more fruitful (John 15:1-2).

Consider This:

Is there an area of your life where God is "pruning" you right now? What is most painful about it? What potential "fruit" do you think it might yield? What Scriptures might encourage you as you get your "fur" yanked or go through your "bald" time? How might you encourage others through their pruning process?

Mew Tube

When Life Makes No Sense, Hanging onto God Does

I know God will not give me anything
I can't handle. I just wish that He
didn't trust me so much.

MOTHER TERESA

We have three grandchildren who live far away from us, so we are very thankful for the wonderful invention of live video streaming. But our precocious black cat, Midnight, doesn't share our gratitude. This new technology seems to confuse her, and she reacts with considerable agitation whenever we use it.

Typically, Midnight hears our voices, enters the room, and begins to meow excitedly as she rubs against our legs. As she rubs, she purrs—a much louder purr than normal. After doing this for a while, she jumps up on my lap, still meowing. But it's not to curl up. Instead, she becomes aggressive. She rubs her face hard against my arms and tries to bite my hands. Then she begins to slap at me. This is the point at which we put her out of the room so we can finish our videoconference in peace. Sometimes she sits outside the door and continues to meow her displeasure. After we hang up, she returns to her normal self.

Midnight acts this way whenever we videoconference. It's the only time she ever does so. We've been puzzled by her behavior. All we can figure is that she's confused by what takes place. She hears the voices of people she knows, but she can't smell them, and it's too much for her little cat brain to handle. She has no way to ask us what's happening, and she's so bothered by her bewilderment that she lashes out.

I've also lashed out at my Master over being confused by what was happening in my life. It was the time of my mother's death, and our then five-year-old daughter Sarah had been affected in a frightening way. Mom lived with us, and she had been ill for over six months. We all knew she was dying, and she was on hospice care. Of course, having someone at death's door affected our whole family. But it hit Sarah in a very physical way. She had diarrhea every day, and her thin frame became much too skinny. One day as I looked at her, I was overcome with fear that there might be something terribly wrong besides her grief.

Finally, the Lord took my mother home to be with Him. We felt relief that her pain was over. I had great peace knowing Mom was with the Lord she loved so much. And I expected Sarah to get well right away. But she didn't.

My fear and agitation grew. I started wondering if the Lord was going to take my daughter home as well. I didn't know what God was doing. I felt as confused about what was happening with Sarah as I think Midnight does about the live video streaming. I struggled in my thoughts and prayers. I acted like Midnight when she hits at me. I lashed out at my Lord. "What are You doing?" I howled. "Mother is fine now. I know that. The suffering has been horrible, but now it's supposed to end. Sarah is supposed to get better, and she's not. You aren't going to take her too, are You?"

After a few days of this behavior, I knew I had to place my trust in my Master. I was able to tell Him, "Even if You take Sarah as well, I'll stay with You because You are the one true God." I think that's what He was waiting to hear. I think God was waiting for me to pass the test of trusting Him even in the midst of confusion. Sarah stopped having diarrhea the very next day and started to put on the weight she'd lost.

Scripture tells us that Job was confused by his circumstances as well. Job 1:1 says he was "blameless and upright; he feared God and shunned evil." He had been blessed with health and wealth and many sons and daughters. Those who lived around him respected him as a great man. Then, he lost it all! As he struggled with his horrific circumstances, he lashed out at God the way I had over Sarah, and the way Midnight had with me. Job cried out, "Your hands shaped me and made me. Will you now turn and destroy me? Remember that you molded me like clay. Will you now turn me to dust again?" (Job 10:8-9).

Job's friends tried to help him, but they failed miserably. Finally Job dialogued at length with God. In his confusion, he drew nearer to God, and had a personal encounter that gave him a whole new understanding of who God is. Job repented of lashing out, telling God, "Surely I spoke of things I did not understand, things too wonderful for me to know…My ears had heard of you but now my eyes have seen you. Therefore I despise myself and repent in dust and ashes" (Job 42:3, 5-6).

Because she's just a kitty, Midnight doesn't know how to trust me in the midst of confusion. So I take her out of the situation to help her. I know what's best for her. God knows what's best for me too. He knows He can grow my faith by using the confusing events of my life to teach me I can place my trust in Him even when I don't understand!

Trust in the Lord *with all your heart and lean not on your own understanding (Proverbs 3:5).*

Consider This:

Was there a time when you were confused about what was happening in your life? Did you turn to God in trust or lash out at Him? How was the situation resolved? What did you learn? Is there an area of confusion you need to surrender to Him right now?

The Cat That Knocked on Hearts
Reach Out and Love

*Where we love is home, home that our
feet may leave, but not our hearts.*

OLIVER WENDELL HOLMES

Connie and Wayne had almost forgotten about their neighbors' little Siamese cat who occasionally came to visit them. Then one cool fall evening she "knocked" on their kitchen screen door. They discovered she'd been left home alone when her human family went on vacation. They had made no arrangements for her food or water.

Connie and Wayne let her in and fed her and played with her. The little cat came back every day. Soon Wayne told Connie he thought the kitty was pregnant. She seemed too young, but it proved to be true. One cold night Connie let her stay inside curled up on the sofa. Early the next morning, Wayne woke his wife and announced, "We are in the kitten business." Sure enough, she'd had her kittens in their closet. Wayne found one of them in his shoe. Since her human family was still gone, Wayne and Connie fixed a box in the bathroom for the little mama and her new babies.

Connie and Wayne were getting pretty attached to this kitty. When they noticed she was acting sick, they took her to the vet. The vet gave them medicine and told them how to treat her. She responded well. By now they were calling her Bluebell because of her beautiful blue eyes. Bluebell knew these humans loved her.

When the neighbors returned from their vacation, Connie told them about Bluebell and her kittens. They didn't seem interested in the kitten news. They didn't offer to pay for their cat's food or vet expenses. They said Connie and Wayne could keep Bluebell…and that is just what happened. Bluebell's new humans kept all three of her kittens too. They loved and nurtured them and all four kitties lived to a ripe old age.

It's not just kitties that may need new families to welcome and nurture them. I know of a family whose adopted twins came to them in this way. The birth father left town, and the birth mother had many problems and couldn't care for her babies. She went to a local church for help. The church knew of this loving couple and asked them to take in these little ones. They loved the twins as their own. Unlike Bluebell's original owners, the twins' biological mother eventually wanted them back. After a long, difficult time, the courts decided to keep the children with their new family instead. The twins knew they were loved and cared for by their adoptive parents. Although there were some problems, they grew up to be loving, responsible adults.

Connie and Wayne and the adoptive parents reached out in love to "orphans" who needed them. God asks all of us to do this, and it can take many forms. It may mean giving financial help to an organization or ministry. It may mean letting your child's friend whose parents work late hang out at your house after school. It may mean some other form of outreach God will lay on your heart. When we do these things it pleases God, because we are being like Him.

God is the perfect parent. He promises that He will never, ever leave or forsake His children. In John 14:18-20, Jesus tells His disciples, "I will not leave you as orphans; I will come to you. Before long, the world will not see me anymore, but you will see me. Because I live, you also will live. On that day you will realize that I am in my Father, and you are in me, and I am in you."

One of the ways God cares for orphans is by laying them on our hearts, as He did with Connie and Wayne and the twins' adoptive parents. Is there an "orphan" knocking on your heart that you might bless?

Here are the kinds of beliefs that God our Father accepts as pure and without fault. When widows and children who have no parents are in trouble, take care of them. And keep yourselves from being polluted by the world (James 1:27, NIrV).

Consider This:

What are some ways that God has shown His love for you as His child? What difference has it made? How might you show that love to an "orphan" in your own church or community? How might you do this for a child somewhere else in the world?

The Final Lap
Seek God

When Jesus comes,
the shadows depart.

AUTHOR UNKNOWN

We have a lot of people living under one roof at the moment. We are often running in different directions, but now and then we get a chance to spend the evening together. On one particular night, after the little ones were in bed, the five adults decided to watch a movie together. We had just settled into our seats and turned on the living room DVD player when we heard the cat door swing open, and in walked Midnight.

Midnight is a cat with attitude. She knows what she wants and goes after her goal until she gets it. This night, she was after a lap. She marched to the middle of the living room rug and peered from face to face, perusing her people. Then she proceeded to jump into a lap. That lap's owner wasn't very receptive (we are not all cat lovers), so she proceeded to a second one. The person who belonged to that lap moaned that she would have a sneezing attack if Midnight stayed too close to her. Midnight, oblivious, curled up there anyway. She looked quite cozy for a couple of minutes, but then she abruptly got up and moved on. Apparently that was not the correct lap, either.

She chose a third lap, curled up, and again seemed quite content. We laughed that Midnight had finally found the lap that suited her. We were wrong. She stayed for only five minutes. This time she jumped down and marched back to the center of the living room to assess her choices once more. Then she deliberately jumped up into my husband's lap, but not to settle there. Instead, she used it as a walkway to get to mine. I was her fifth choice, but my lap was the one that ended Midnight's search. She curled up happily and remained there for the entire two-hour movie. She had found the lap for which she'd been searching.

The next day, as I pondered Midnight's quest for the right lap, I thought about one of my dearest friends, Melissa. I met her 25 years ago when she joined my Bible study class. She was a new believer, and I loved her great enthusiasm for the Lord, which she shared with everyone. She'd been searching for spiritual truth the way Midnight had been searching for the right lap, and she had finally found it in Jesus.

Melissa's seeking had taken her to all sorts of other places first. Someone at the airport invited her to attend his meeting, so off she went. She found clear non-truth there, so she didn't stay. She tried a popular Eastern belief system for a while, but that didn't sit right either. As Melissa got into each religion, she gave it her all. She said, "I tried each one out with all my heart, but there were clear discrepancies." Melissa was going from lap to lap to find the one with truth, but none of them held up in the end.

After all this unsuccessful lap-hopping, she developed an urgent problem; she was heading for a divorce. She knew she needed a miracle to save her marriage, and she knew that Christians were always claiming to have them, so she started visiting a Christian church. There she met the One who said, "I am the way and the truth and the life" (John 14:6). Finally she'd found the lap she'd been searching for. This was the one in which she would stay. Sadly, her marriage wasn't saved; but she was. She got a different kind of miracle…that of beginning a personal relationship with the true and living God.

Once Melissa asked Jesus into her life, her questions found answers. She hadn't known it was possible to be in a relationship with God, since He was beyond our thinking. Then she learned that God sent His Son to earth to live among us as a human, and He was the bridge to God.

She hadn't known all her sins could be forgiven. She learned that Jesus purchased her forgiveness by dying in her place as a sinless sacrifice. She hadn't known she could be sure she would go to heaven when she died. Then she found out it was her faith in Jesus that guarantees heaven: "Whoever believes in the Son has eternal life" (John 3:36).

The Ethiopian eunuch was looking for the right "lap" too (Acts 8:27-40). He had gone to worship in Jerusalem. On his way home he was reading the Old Testament book of Isaiah. God sent a prominent believer named Philip to join him in his chariot and tell him about Jesus. The Ethiopian realized he'd found the lap he was seeking and was baptized right then and there.

Midnight's quest for just the right lap was random and capricious. Not Melissa's. Hers was intentional, like the Ethiopian seeker. She was searching for God and tried all sorts of laps until she found Him. She was sincere and she didn't give up. She says now that the more she studies the Bible, the more she understands God's plan to call everyone into His lap through Jesus so they can become His children. She's glad she took the time to seek, because now that she is settled there she will stay safely curled up in God's lap forever!

You will seek me and find me when you seek me with all your heart (Jeremiah 29:13).

Consider This:

Have you found a personal relationship with God, or are you still seeking the right "lap?" If you are searching, have you asked God to show you what's true? If you know others who are seeking, have you thought of inviting them to your church or Bible study?

The Ultimate Fixer
Love Heals

*Healing is a matter of time, but it is
sometimes also a matter of opportunity.*

HIPPOCRATES

Cats weren't really Tom's and Nora's favorite thing, but Fixer "fixed" that. They first heard the little cat meowing loudly outside their office. She didn't have a name then, and she didn't have a home either. But she also didn't seem to be in trouble. Their location was near a restaurant. Many cats roamed the area, feasting on the contents of the garbage cans. But Tom knew Nora's propensity to care for all of God's creation. He told her he figured she'd buy food for the cat, so why wait?

Sure enough, Nora did try to feed the kitty. But the little cat remained afraid of them. Then one morning they heard loud, concerning noises. They went out to search and soon found the kitty, badly beaten up. She was bloody and very dirty and in great need of help and love. They picked her up carefully and took her to a veterinarian.

Even though she was in pretty bad shape, the vet thought that with care, the little cat would make it. Tom and Nora were willing to help. They took her home and hoped she'd become a member of their family.

Tom decided to name her "Fixer" because that was part of the name of their business.

Fixer got well from her physical wounds, but she was still leery of Tom and Nora. She wasn't "fixed" emotionally yet. She lived outside and would not come near them. They kept leaving food for her and after a while she finally ventured up to their door and ate the tasty provisions.

Tom and Nora kept reaching out to Fixer. After much time and coaxing and prayer, she became a sweet, calm family member. She has her own special place to sleep, and also curls up on the office sofas. Tom and Nora meet her needs and keep her comfortable and protected.

Healing happened on both sides. Fixer's new family helped heal her fear of people as well as her physical wounds. But Fixer fixed their outlook on cats. They both love her—and so does anyone who comes to their office. I spent a short while with Fixer, and I grew to love her too.

When I was a little girl, I needed some fixing as well. We lived in a small town, in a quiet little neighborhood right out of a 1950s television show. We had a new neighbor who seemed old and scary to me. I didn't want to go near her house. When I had to pass by, I would walk in the middle of the street to stay farther away.

My mother must have realized my fear of this neighbor needed fixing. One day she said, "Connie, why don't you go sweep Mrs. Olgesby's sidewalk? She is old and crippled and I know that would make her very happy. I'm sure you would feel good about it as well—and so would Jesus."

I was all for making Jesus happy, but I wasn't sure about the rest of it. I solemnly started sweeping our sidewalk with our straw broom. I kept sweeping as I made my way in front of Mrs. Olgesby's home. Just as I was finishing, she came out of her house. This was the worst thing I could imagine. I wanted to run. But she called to me to come and talk to her. My face fell. I met her halfway and she put both her hands on my shoulders. She asked me why I had swept her sidewalk. I said I thought she would like it. She looked down at me and gave me a huge smile. Her "scary" face transformed into the visage of a brightly smiling old grandma. Happy tears dripped from her eyes as she told me this was one of the nicest things anyone had ever done for her.

Mrs. Olgesby and I became friends that day. I not only stopped avoiding her house, but she invited me in for milk and cookies and told me stories about her childhood. She fixed my fear of old people and I helped fix her fears about noisy little kids—just like Tom and Nora and their cat would help fix each other so many years later.

It's important to reach out and heal when we have the opportunity, but we can't fix it all. Fortunately, God can do what we can't. He is the ultimate Fixer and Healer. Jesus, God's Son, fixed mankind's sin problem with His sacrificial death on the cross. And while He ministered on this earth, He constantly reached out to those deemed "unfixable" with His healing touch.

Jesus even "fixed" one who tried to arrest Him. When a crowd seized Him in Gethsemane, Peter grabbed a sword and cut off one man's ear. Jesus restored and healed the ear and told Peter, "No more of this!" (Luke 22:51). Jesus not only fixed the man's wound, He sought to fix Peter's perspective. And though we don't know, perhaps this helped bring the man to faith and heal him spiritually for eternity.

Tom and Nora showed love to Fixer. I showed love to Mrs. Olgesby. Jesus showed love to a wounded enemy and died for us while we were still enemies of His. Love was the fixer, and God's redeeming love is the greatest gift and fixer of all!

My command is this: Love each other as I have loved you. Greater love has no one than this: to lay down one's life for one's friends (John 15:12-13).

Consider This:

Have you ever been "fixed" by love? Who reached out to you? What happened? How did it change your life? Is there someone God might want to heal through your love?

Chickadee in Charge
God Builds Our Trust

*Don't trust to hold God's hand; let
Him hold yours. Let Him do the
holding, and you the trusting.*

HAMMER WILLIAM WEBB-PEPLOE

I've heard it said that being laid-back seems characteristic of orange cats. I don't know if that's truth or myth, but Bonco could have furthered the perception. He was a marvelous orange and white kitty who "owned" my mom for a number of years. He was also a sensible fellow who knew when to kick back and go with the flow, even when the "flow" came in the shape of an energetic black and white dog.

This dog's name was Chickadee and she was a Peke-a-poo…part Pekinese and part poodle. She loved to play with her kitty pal, but she wanted to do it on her terms. Chickadee's terms were to grab Bonco by the scruff of his neck and drag him around. I don't know exactly how this got started. But I do know that at some point, Bonco must have learned to trust his furry playmate's intentions. He didn't run or fight. He didn't get all hot and bothered. He just kicked back, let her pull him around, and enjoyed the ride. He'd figured out she wouldn't hurt him and her antics were no skin off his fur. So he put himself in her paws (or more accurately, her mouth) and let her do her thing.

How different my personality is from Bonco's! If I'd been born a cat and some dog tried to drag me, I'd have lost it. I'd have flown in the air, claws out, fur on end, shrieking fit to shatter glass! The doctor who delivered me told Mom I was a worrier by nature. Worriers don't kick back and let themselves get pulled along by other people or life events or even the Lord. Fortunately, the God who made me knows me even better than that doctor did, and in His infinitely patient and loving way has worked with me over decades to teach me to entrust myself to Him.

One small stepping-stone in that journey was my dental implant surgery. I had damaged some teeth as a teen, and over the years a couple had gone bad and had to be extracted. My dentist thought I might be a good candidate for dental implants, and sent me to a colleague skilled in this procedure. He agreed.

Positive as my prospects seemed, I felt daunted. I have some minor health blips that give me cardiac-type symptoms from time to time. I've also had a lifelong fear of death. Even though I had medical clearance to do the implants and my friends were praying, I was scared. I agreed to put myself in my dental surgeon's hands, and God's. But instead of being limp and relaxed, like Bonco was with Chickadee, I was rigid with apprehension. In fact, I'd opted for a type of anesthesia that allows the patient to stay partially conscious because I feared if I was put totally under, I might not wake up.

My loving Lord understood, and He was gentle with me as He used even this life event to build my trust. He gave my best friend a special Bible verse for me. All these years later I don't remember what it was, but I do remember how perfectly it fit and eased my nerves.

Nonetheless, I still felt traumatized in the dental chair as I was about to begin the procedure. My dental surgeon asked how I was doing, and I admitted to being anxious. What he said next broke the tension and made me grin inside. He told me the anesthesia I'd be receiving was actually what they gave to patients suffering from anxiety attacks!

Looking back, I believe God knew how to comfort me not only from His Word but also from my doctor's mouth. I kicked back in the dental chair and allowed my physician and my Great Physician to pull me through the required surgery. It went beautifully, I healed swiftly, and the implants have been a blessing. And this experience deepened my faith and trust in God.

God gave the Israelites of old many experiences to prove that they were safe in His hands. He led them out of Egypt and into the Promised Land. He gave them victory over a whole host of enemies. To encourage them to remember that they could put themselves in His hands, He commanded them to keep special commemorative festivals to remind them of His love and care.

Bonco was mellow, but he was no dummy. I'm guessing if some other dog had tried Chickadee's stunt, he might not have allowed it. But he'd built a relationship with that dog over time, and his experience had taught him he was safe with her.

God wants to build a relationship with us. He wants to show us we are safe with Him. Will you step out in faith and place yourself in His hands, so He can show His faithfulness to you?

Celebrate the Feast of Unleavened Bread, because it was on this very day that I brought your divisions out of Egypt. Celebrate this day as a lasting ordinance for the generations to come (Exodus 12:17).

Consider This:

What life experiences has God used to build your trust in Him? In what areas do you still struggle to put yourself in His hands? What step of faith might He want you to take so He can increase your trust even more?

Wild or Wooed?

Love Transforms

I love you not only for what you are, but for
what I am when I am with you. I love you
not only for what you have made of yourself,
but for what you are making of me. I love
you for the part of me that you bring out.

ROY CROFT

My friend Stephanie learned a lot from a cat she named Scruffy. He was quite shabby and dirty when she first saw him—thus the name. He may well have been born in the wild because he was frightened by human contact. He only came to Stephanie's house for food. Her family had several cats they fed on the porch, so Scruffy joined them for breakfast and dinner.

When Stephanie first reached out to Scruffy, all she got for her trouble was a scratch on the hand. She was more careful the next time, but he still snarled at her. Stephanie continued to feed Scruffy, and while he ate she talked softly to him.

Stephanie wanted to love Scruffy into health. She knew it would take time, so she didn't push him. She was committed to loving him without getting anything in return, but she hoped someday her love would transform him into a sweet kitty friend. After a month of talking gently to him as he ate, she tried to touch him again. This time he gave a low growl but didn't scratch her. She was encouraged. She was seeing how love—selfless love—works.

It was tough waiting, but after a few months, Scruffy actually seemed happy to see Stephanie herself, and not just his meal. She had allowed him to progress at his own pace, and it paid off. The next time she reached out to pet him, he didn't growl at her touch. Little by little Scruffy accepted her love and finally began to return it. By the time a year had rolled around, this pretty kitty had become the sweet loving pal that Stephanie had longed for when she first met him.

My son Sam and his wife Andrea went through a similar experience during their first year of marriage. Andrea was a lovely girl, and when Sam first brought her home to meet the family, we instantly fell in love with her, just as he had. We knew that her childhood had been rather nightmarish, but we didn't know it would have serious repercussions for their relationship.

However, that's exactly what happened during that first year after their wedding. When Andrea was upset, she would strike out in anger at Sam and threaten to leave him. She actually did leave a couple of times. She fled to her best friend's home. Fortunately, that wise woman drove her back to Sam each time—explaining that marriage was a solemn vow and Andrea needed to stick it out while she worked through her problems.

Sam's response to Andrea's brokenness was to love her unconditionally in spite of his hurt. He put her needs ahead of his, just as Stephanie put Scruffy's needs above her own. Sam repeatedly told his wife that no matter what happened he would not abandon her, as others had in her childhood. He told her that despite her parents' broken marriages, theirs was a marriage that would last a lifetime. He told her that the wall she'd thrown up out of hurt and necessity could be taken down—but he didn't try to force it down. He allowed her to proceed on her own timetable. He just continued to love her into health.

As Andrea began to realize the damage her childhood had done to her, she got tearful and angry at times. Sam absorbed the anger and returned love instead. Over and over he told her he would never stop loving her—and in so doing displayed the unconditional love God has for her and all His children. Each time Sam did this, Andrea softened, her wall came down further, and she grew more secure in both Sam's love and God's.

That first year was quite difficult, but slowly Andrea began to believe Sam. Because of his loyal, persistent love, her defensive wall continued to come down. Finally it was shattered altogether. Andrea was made whole through the unconditional love Sam lived out for her. Just as Scruffy had been transformed into a sweet kitty, so Andrea's life took on a marvelous sweetness as love healed her heart.

The great apostle Paul was also transformed by God's love. He'd been filled with hatred for the new movement called "The Way." He was a Pharisee, a member of Israel's religious elite, and he was intent on ridding the world of this new "sect" which would soon be called Christianity.

Unlike Scruffy and Andrea, Paul was changed in an instant by meeting God in a blinding light. God's love remade him into an apostle who would write much of the New Testament. Paul was still a Jew, but one who now understood God's plan of reconciliation for all peoples. He spent the rest of his life trying to reach both Jews and Gentiles with the gospel message. He was rejected, persecuted, beaten, imprisoned, and finally martyred. But he returned love for hatred and urged all God's children to do likewise. Paul wrote, "As God's chosen people, holy and dearly loved, clothe yourselves with compassion, kindness, humility, gentleness and patience. Bear with each other and forgive one another if any of you has a grievance against someone. Forgive as the Lord forgave you. And over all these virtues put on love, which binds them all together in perfect unity" (Colossians 3:12-14).

Scruffy, Andrea, and Paul demonstrate the transforming power of love—especially God's unconditional love. God's love can transform you too, if you will allow Him to draw you near and heal you with His loving care.

For I am convinced that neither death nor life, neither angels nor demons, neither the present nor the future, nor any powers, neither height nor depth, nor anything else in all creation, will be able to separate us from the love of God that is in Christ Jesus our Lord (Romans 8:38-39).

Consider This:

Do you have a Scruffy or Andrea in your life? Have they kept you at a distance or lashed out because of past hurts? How have you responded? Do you have a protective wall that needs to come down? Have you asked God for help in this area?

"Cattitude" Adjustment
Love Is Patient

*Patience and Diligence, like
faith, remove mountains.*

WILLIAM PENN

Pele was a beautiful Siamese cat who deigned to let humans named Rosie and Ernie share his dwelling. He also let them feed and care for him. He had special kitty food, mostly fish because that was his favorite. He had a wonderfully comfortable cat bed in the library where his people spent a good portion of their time. He also liked sitting in their laps when he felt like it. But if they called him and he wasn't interested, there was no chance he would oblige.

Pele was a feline with "cattitude," and it got worse from there. He had a habit of breaking precious things. Rosie was an avid collector, and her home was filled with fine china, glass, and canvas art. Pele seemed to know which pieces were most precious to Rosie and sought them out. He would climb a high shelf, walk on narrow pieces of wood, do anything it took to reach them. He seemed to be on a mission to knock down and destroy everything she valued. This made Rosie furious. At times she would cry because her special pieces meant a great deal to her—regardless of their monetary value. But Pele kept right on doing what he was doing.

Rosie and Ernie could have gotten rid of Pele, but they didn't. Because they loved him, they forgave him. They patiently cleaned up each mess as it occurred and went on with their lives. Once Pele even climbed up on the headboard of their bed and knocked a water glass onto Rosie's head. Was it intentional? No one really knows. But it felt that way to Rosie. Not only did the glass knick her head, but her heart was wounded. Her cat seemed intent on showing animosity toward her. Yet Rosie kept on pardoning Pele, hoping that in time she would have a more positive relationship with her "bad cattitude" feline.

It took years, but Pele finally responded to this patient love and forgiveness. He came around to loving his humans back. He quit breaking precious things and settled down into a lazy, relaxed kitty who enjoyed being on his people's laps and receiving their affection.

Human children may also "break" what their parents value most. I remember going through hard times with friends of ours whose son had decided to take the wrong path in his young life. Grant had grown up in the church. He knew Jesus as his personal Savior. But he started hanging with friends who drank and did drugs, and he chose to follow their example. He even stole from his parents to pay for his bad habits. He broke their hearts as well as their trust in him.

My husband Steve and I, along with many other friends, prayed earnestly for Grant to come back to the Lord. Like Pele the cat, he kept up his destructive ways for some time. But, after a long hard road for everyone, Grant realized he was messing up his life pretty badly. He got tired of hurting his parents. He talked to them and asked for their forgiveness. He prayed to the Lord for forgiveness, too. We know that God forgave him, but his parents did as well, welcoming him home with open arms. It took lots of hard work and there were trials to overcome, but Grant has grown into a strong Christian man who loves the Lord and seeks to serve Him. Grant is grateful every day that those who love him refused to give up on him—just like Ernie and Rosie refused to give up on Pele.

God's children have broken His heart too—individually and collectively. In Matthew 23:37, Jesus lamented, "Jerusalem, Jerusalem, you who kill the prophets and stone those sent to you, how often I have longed to gather your children together, as a hen gathers her chicks under her wings, but you were not willing." The Old Testament is filled with examples of the Israelites turning to idolatry and breaking the heart and trust of the God who had delivered them. Plenty of New Testament Gentile and Jewish believers stumbled too, deeply paining God and also the apostle Paul, as his letters show. But God's patient love will not give up on us, either.

It took a lot for Rosie and Ernie to forgive their "bad cattitude" kitty. It took far more for Grant's parents to forgive him. It took the death of God's Son, our Messiah, for our Father in heaven to purchase our redemption. But just as Pele was precious to his humans and just as Grant was precious to his parents, we are precious to our loving Father in heaven. He knows the worst breakage from our sin is us. We are destroying ourselves. Will you allow Him to adjust your "cattitude" and draw you into His loving lap?

He is patient with you, not wanting anyone to perish, but everyone to come to repentance (2 Peter 3:9).

Consider This:

Is there someone who has consistently wounded you and "broken" what you hold precious? Have you continued to love and forgive that person? If so, how has he or she responded? If not, are you willing to pray and ask God to empower you to do so?

Part II

Climbing up God's Path

BO

You Can Lead a Cat to Water But...

God's Spirit Gives Life

We never know the worth of
water till the well is dry.

THOMAS FULLER

My cat Bo drinks water like no other kitty I have ever seen. It's as though he's giving his water bowl a hug. He wraps his paws around it, sticks his head in, and laps up the life-giving liquid. Bo needs that water to keep him alive and healthy. But he's an indoor cat, and he can't get it for himself. He depends on me, his master, to provide this vital drink without which he could not survive.

Barney and Misty were cats that depended on me for water in a whole different way. They had reached an advanced age and their kidneys weren't working properly. They couldn't drink enough water by mouth to satisfy their bodies' needs. Their vet taught me how to help them take in extra water through a drip under the skin several times a week.

I also learned how to tell if my cats were dehydrated. If their bodies had too little water and I pinched a small amount of fur, it would remain sticking up instead of falling softly back into place. That danger sign would alert me that my kitties were getting into trouble.

Just as water sustains physical life, God's Holy Spirit sustains us spiritually. Jesus used water as a metaphor for the Spirit. After asking the Samaritan woman at the well for a drink (John 4), He said, "If you knew the gift of God and who it is that asks you for a drink, you would have asked him and he would have given you living water" (John 4:10). Jesus went on to explain that anyone who drank physical earthly water would eventually become thirsty again, but "whoever drinks the water I give them will never thirst. Indeed, the water I give them will become in them a spring of water welling up to eternal life" (John 4:14).

Just as I give my kitties water, my Master has given me His Spirit. The Bible says we receive the Holy Spirit when we trust in Jesus' death on the cross for our salvation and give our hearts to Him. But it is possible to quench the ministry of the Spirit in our lives, leading to a kind of spiritual dehydration. That's what I did when I lost my beloved dog Morgan.

Morgan was snatched from me on an awful September night. He disappeared from my fenced yard without a trace. I was shocked to learn a coyote could get over my six-foot fencing. The best guess was that Morgan had been grabbed by one. This dog had been my soul mate for years and at first, I couldn't come to terms with what had happened. I lived on a knife-edge of bitterness toward God. I didn't fully realize where my heart was, but I unwittingly revealed it to my best friend and coauthor Dottie. In the midst of my searing pain, I blurted, "I feel like God is mean."

Dottie saw the signs of my "spiritual dehydration," and she took action. She gently warned me I was on dangerous ground. "You can be angry at God. You can question Him," she told me. "But if you say that God is mean, you're attributing evil to God, which we must never do."

Those words got me very upset with my dearest friend. But I also knew Dottie was right. In my heart I had been attacking God's character. I needed intervention, and her loving warning functioned as a sort of spiritual dehydration test. I poured out my heart to God in prayer. I expressed my pain and hurt, but I also confessed and repented of attributing meanness to my good, merciful, and loving Father. And it was at that moment that my healing from Morgan's loss began.

Months later, I believe my confession released the Spirit to work in my life and begin rehydrating me spiritually. I still sobbed and grieved, but a certain sharp cutting edge of that grief was gone. Six months afterward, I saw fresh evidence of that rehydration when I got a call out of the blue from someone who had found Morgan's collar. It was in an area where a coyote could easily have carried him. It was closed as if still around his neck. I could have been ripped apart, but God's rehydration process covered even this. I'd surrendered to God. I stayed surrendered. And God protected my heart.

Bo still laps water freely from his bowl each day. But there are times when my sin keeps God's Spirit from flowing freely in my life. I am grateful that when that happens, I can confess and turn from my error and He will restore me to healthy hydration in Him.

And do not grieve the Holy Spirit of God, with whom you were sealed for the day of redemption (Ephesians 4:30).

Consider This:

Has there been a time when you felt spiritually dehydrated? What do you think caused the problem? What effect did it have? If you became rehydrated, how did that happen? If not, is there something you need to repent of so the Spirit can flow freely again?

Moberly Standard Time
Be Flexible for God

*Prepare yourself for the world, as the
athletes used to do for their exercise;
oil your mind and your manners, to
give them the necessary suppleness and
flexibility; strength alone will not do.*

LORD CHESTERFIELD

Moberly didn't consider variety the spice of life. This little calico cat craved structure. That's why living with her first human, my friend Martha, didn't quite suit her. Martha worked in the news business and her hours could be quite irregular. Getting home late got Moberly's fur in a fluff. She was quick to show her displeasure. One of the ways she acted out was to use Martha's shoes as a litter box. There was no way to explain to a cat why a news person's life couldn't happen on "Moberly Standard Time," so the pair were at a standoff.

Martha would have lived with Moberly's sometimes messy foibles, but her circumstances changed and she couldn't keep a cat any longer. Moberly found a new home with Martha's mom. This was the life of Moberly's dreams. Her new person got up at the same time five days a week to go to work and returned at about the same time each night.

Her weekend schedule was fairly predictable too. Ahhh—blissful regularity—almost!

Truth be told, there was still one tiny fly in Moberly's mackerel (her favorite food). Every so often, Martha's mom had a three-day weekend. Moberly apparently somehow knew the difference between two lazier mornings and three—and wasn't about to let sleeping elderly ladies lie! Maybe this cat's fur was soft, but her will was steel, and she soon found a means of having her way with her human.

Martha's mom loved collectibles. She had charming, delicate vases, figurines, and other breakables. Some of them were lovingly arranged on her bedroom dresser. When she dared linger in bed on the third day of a delicious long weekend, Moberly sprang into action. She leaped to the top of the chest and deliberately batted those collectibles with her paw, nudging them closer and closer to the edge.

Moberly never actually knocked any knickknacks over the side of that chest. She didn't have to. The scraping sound they made as she nudged them, and her human's fear of the breakage, fully accomplished Moberly's purpose. Martha's mom caved, launched out of bed—and Moberly's regularity was restored.

Moberly's refusal to go with the flow of her human's schedule seems funny now. But what would happen if we acted like this cat? What might we miss if our heavenly Master tried to hand us a schedule-bending new ministry opportunity, and we clung to our old, safe ways instead of joining Him on the adventure?

That's exactly what happened to my friend and coauthor Dottie. Dottie loves being on an early to bed, early to rise routine. She is a morning person and her sleep needs are better met this way. She is also a mom and grandma who finds it easier to grab quiet moments with God before the rest of her household climbs out of bed. She loves watching the sunrise with a cup of coffee and a Bible beside her. She is more than happy to turn in at 8 PM. But at times God has other plans, and she has had to decide if she is willing to be flexible for Him.

Dottie has been a Bible teacher for over two decades. For years, she co-taught a morning Bible study class. Then God called her to help start an evening class— one that wouldn't even finish until 8:30 at night. It was a stretch, but Dottie loves God and understood this was His will.

Rather than cling to "Dottie Standard Time," she chose "Jesus Savings Time." She began teaching the evening class. That was 15 years ago. It is still going strong, and has been a huge blessing to its members and to Dottie. Her flexibility has paid big spiritual dividends.

Scripture has many examples of how God turned people's time-tables upside down. Perhaps the most dramatic instance involved a young girl named Mary. She was betrothed to a man named Joseph. In those days, the engagement period lasted a year. During that time, the woman continued to live with her family, and her fiancé built a room for them onto his own parents' home. Only after this betrothal period could the couple move in together and consummate their marriage.

But God had a different timetable for this couple. He was inviting them on an unprecedented schedule-bending new ministry opportunity. Mary got pregnant by the Holy Spirit with God's Son, the promised Messiah. When Joseph learned that she was pregnant, he decided to quietly end the betrothal, thinking she had been unfaithful. Then an angel of the Lord came to him in a dream and clued him in. Would Joseph "flex" with God's timing?

Resoundingly…yes! Joseph took Mary as his wife and received the incomparable privilege of helping to raise the Savior of mankind.

Moberly didn't understand the reason for her master's change of timing. We often don't know just what God is up to either—at least not right away. But we know His thoughts and ways are perfect—unlike ours! If we hold our schedules loosely and go with His flow, who knows how He may choose to bless and use us for His purposes and glory!

But after he had considered this, an angel of the Lord appeared to him in a dream and said, "Joseph son of David, do not be afraid to take Mary home as your wife, because what is conceived in her is from the Holy Spirit. She will give birth to a son, and you are to give him the name Jesus, because he will save his people from their sins" (Matthew 1:20-21).

Consider This:

When was the last time your preferred schedule got turned upside down? Did you cling to "Moberly Standard Time" or go with the flow? If you were flexible, did it serve God's purposes? How?

A Bag of Kitties
and a Duffel Bag of Hope

Love Uplifts

A loving heart is the beginning of all knowledge.

THOMAS CARLYLE

As I was visiting a dear old friend from my high school days, she shared a story about some "throw-away" kittens. Her children found them in a bag in the alley—tossed out like garbage. They knew these little ones wouldn't survive unless they brought them to Mom. She took the bag inside and gently unwrapped the kittens from the loose-weave burlap.

There were five kittens to start. They appeared to be only a few days old and still had their eyes closed. My friend called the vet and he said to bring them in immediately. As the doctor was checking them over, one little guy gave up. It was sad to see him pass away. Though the others were tiny, starving, and sick, the vet thought there might be a chance to save them.

My friend decided to try. She bought the necessary formula and bottles and whatever else the vet suggested. He told her he wouldn't charge her for the appointment. She was giving her time and love to these sad little homeless babies and he felt charging her would be wrong. She took the needed supplies, the kittens, and her children home and everyone worked at getting the tiny creatures comfortable for the night. Later that evening one more tiny kitten lost its struggle for life. The next morning they buried it in the backyard with a little ceremony.

It took love and perseverance on the family's part, but the other kittens survived. The kids helped raise them to be beautiful, loving pets. They sat on their people's laps and played silly games with yarn and small bouncing balls. Saving the kittens became a wonderful lesson about serving others and showing them God's love.

In the beginning these kittens were treated as refuse. It took a caring, loving person to lift them out of their filthy rags, feed and nurture them, and help them not only survive, but thrive. My friend did that for those kitties. My mom did that for people.

When I was growing up, our home was always open to folks who needed a place to rest. Often these were guys who were my brother's friends. One young man in particular often came to our house when he was tired, hungry, dirty, and needed a mom.

One time Mom wasn't home when Pete showed up with his duffel bag of dirty clothes. Now my dad was a farmer and dirt was no stranger to our home. But this dirt was different. It was from homeless living. Being a teenager, I didn't realize how shallow my "unlimited" knowledge was. I didn't see how far off my values were. I told Pete I didn't want to do his laundry because I was sure it was too dirty to put in our washing machine.

I'll never forget the look of hurt and rejection in Pete's eyes. I realized then that Mom would have taken care of everything without even thinking. She would have hugged him, washed his clothes, and made him a good meal. Just as my friend's love for homeless kittens would teach her children more about love years later, Mom's example showed me that my knowledge had room to grow, and so did my heart. I apologized to Pete, washed his clothes, and made dinner. When my parents came home we all enjoyed the meal I'd cooked and listened to his stories of the places he'd been, the things he'd done, and what he still hoped to accomplish.

When Pete left the next morning, he hugged me and told me he loved me and how grateful he was that I was his "little sister." I was grateful for him, too, as I hugged him back. Just as the kittens' new family would take them out of their dirty bag to love them, I learned to separate my friend from his dirty duffel bag and care about him. That day I learned that love was more important than dirty clothes. I learned how my mom's love for others made the world a brighter and lighter place. Once again, Mom taught me how to love the Lord and serve Him by helping and loving others in obedience to Him.

Jesus constantly reached out to love and rescue those whom others considered discards. These included lepers, who in those days had to live away from society and call out "Unclean, unclean!" so people knew to avoid them. Luke 17:11-19 records how ten lepers approached the Lord and pleaded for mercy. He healed them all. Only one, a Samaritan, came back to thank Him. Knowing all things, He knew that would happen, but He reached out with His healing touch to the other nine despite this. He also reached out to those considered spiritually and socially unclean. When self-righteous religious leaders condemned His kindness, He replied, "It is not the healthy who need a doctor, but the sick. I have not come to call the righteous, but sinners to repentance" (Luke 5:31-32).

Like the kittens and Pete and those lepers, there may be people God brings into our lives that we may be tempted to shun. If we are willing and obey Him instead, He will use us to give them hope and help them experience His love. And He will use them to help us learn lessons of love, perseverance, and acceptance.

Be devoted to one another in love. Honor one another above yourselves (Romans 12:10).

Consider This:

Have you ever felt God calling you to love someone you preferred to avoid? What did you do? What was the result? Have you ever been hard to love? Did someone reach out anyway? How did God use that in each of your lives?

Older than the Hills

Believe God, Not Your Mirror

*As we advance in life it becomes more and
more difficult, but in fighting the difficulties
the inmost strength of the heart is developed.*

VINCENT VAN GOGH

Midnight is probably the most photographed kitty I've ever had—thanks to being both amusing and beautiful. But she wasn't much to look at when we found her 14 years ago. She was a scraggly little thing when she showed up on our backyard hill at about four weeks of age. However, with proper food and a nice home, she grew into a cat with the most luxurious coat I had ever seen. Her jet-black fur just begged us to dig our fingers into it. Even our veterinarian noticed it. He said it was "like a mink coat." And on her underbelly the rich black fur glistened with lovely golden-brown hues.

Her fur is still thick, silky, and soft to the touch, but the color is quite different. Instead of the gorgeous rich black fur she used to have, her fur has turned brown on her shoulders and back. But it's not the golden brown of her belly. Instead, it's a dull brown everywhere but on her head and legs, which looks completely out of place. When I noticed this happening, I could hardly believe it. Was this an aging phenomenon? Did her black turn to brown from a loss of pigment the way human hair turns gray? I don't know and the veterinarian I asked didn't either, but it reminds me that she won't be with me for my whole life, and that is a sad thought. She just doesn't look like the young, vibrant kitty that stole my heart, even though she still acts the same. I've decided it's the first side effect of growing old.

She's not the only one dealing with aging, either. Like it or not, and it's usually the latter, I'm getting up there too. I see deep lines around my mouth and eyes that I can no longer conceal with makeup. Sometimes my skin even looks like a cross-stitch, and there are indentations where it used to be smooth. My hair is fading and appears dull, kind of like Midnight's new brown. I must add color to make it look vibrant and cover the gray around my temples. Sometimes when I walk by a mirror I wonder who that old woman is! It's a shock to think that I am getting old like my mother and grandmother. This wasn't ever supposed to happen to me. And my body…well, we won't even go there! Then my fears begin. Will I become invisible to society? Will I be discounted because of age? Will I have any value as I grow older?

Years ago my husband and I went to our son's Christian college for a visit. We brought two friends with us who were in their eighties. They'd become family to our kids. When they expressed a desire to see our son's campus, we made a day of it. As we walked slowly along with these precious seniors, the young people on this campus smiled and greeted them graciously. Our friends later shared that this had been a completely unique and wonderful experience. When we asked why, they explained that in their daily life they had grown accustomed to being ignored, so all the attention felt different…and amazingly good. Our society is not one which is kind to the elderly. Japan does better. They have designated one day of the year "respect for the aged day." They honor their elderly and show them love and respect, the way I still do for Midnight.

Though our culture may make us think if we're old we should be out to pasture, God doesn't view us that way. He doesn't value us any less when we age. He doesn't judge us by our fading exterior. He doesn't set a mandatory or even voluntary retirement time. God sees our hearts and can use us mightily at any point in our lives. He didn't retire Moses at the age of 65; instead, He called him into ministry at the ripe old age of 80. Abraham was another oldie but goodie. God called him to leave his homeland when he was 70 to begin the nation of Israel. That's the Old Testament, you say, when people lived longer! Ah, but John the apostle is said to have lived into his nineties, still instructing the church until his death. Anna was "very old" when she greeted Joseph and Mary at the temple as they brought Jesus there. She had worshiped God day and night and now proclaimed that Jesus was to bring redemption!

There are people who have found deep purpose even when age has ravaged their health. I know of women confined to beds in nursing homes who have felt a call from the Lord to pray for the worldwide church. They do this for hours, as they lift up country after country. I know others who communicate with inmates on a regular basis, instructing them in the ways of the Lord. I have an aunt who has been confined to an assisted living facility for years, who found her purpose in telling people about Jesus before they died.

Midnight's value isn't in her looks. My love for her hasn't diminished, in spite of her age. In the same way, my value must not be tied to my age, even in our youth-worshiping culture. Instead, value must be determined by what God thinks of us. After all, He can use anyone who is available.

Even though age has changed Midnight's "outside," she's still the same wonderful kitty I love. She still thrills me as she purrs in my lap and delights me when she plays with a grasshopper. And just as she still blesses me, I can still bless my Master, no matter my age—by serving His purpose and glorifying Him.

The righteous will flourish like a palm tree, they will grow like a cedar of Lebanon; planted in the house of the Lord, they will flourish in the courts of our God. They will still bear fruit in old age, they will stay fresh and green, proclaiming, "The Lord is upright; he is my Rock, and there is no wickedness in him" (Psalm 92:12-15).

Consider This:

How have you bought into our culture's youth worship? Has it affected how you think of older people? Has it impacted your view of your own potential usefulness as you get older? Do you think God may want to adjust your viewpoint? In what way?

Catch of the Day
God Sets Us Free

Freedom has a thousand charms to show,
That slaves, howe'er contented, never know.

WILLIAM COWPER

It was a beautiful winter morning in Yucca Valley, California. Snow had blanketed the ground. My friend Cindy had gotten up early because she was moving and had lots to do. Then something captured her attention—a cat that was sitting across the street, literally out in the cold. It was black with a white face and paws. She felt a surge of anger. How could someone let that kitty roam loose? Not only was it freezing weather, but this desert area was home to prowling coyotes that would happily make lunch out of a defenseless feline.

Cindy tried to approach the cat, but it bolted away in fear. She decided to go door to door. She was hoping to find the cat's owners, but nobody claimed it. All through that day, she kept seeing the furry little orphan.

Cindy has a huge heart for animals and rescues many. As night approached, she resolved to take action. She put a crate out in the snow with a blanket on top and cat food inside. It worked. She caught the little guy and named him Frost.

Frost was feral, but he wasn't aggressive—just leery. Gradually Cindy won his trust. Today he lives in a wonderful climate-controlled cattery she built at her new home. He has plenty of good food to eat, perches to climb on, and scratch pads and toys to amuse and stimulate him. And when Cindy approaches, he doesn't bolt—he rubs against her. He lets her kiss and pet him. He even let Cindy get him vaccinated and neutered. He never tries to escape. He is grateful that this loving human caught him to free him from a life of hunger, cold, and danger...and he wants to stay "captured" forever.

Frost the orphan had no idea that his street life was a prison of cold and want. He didn't realize that in bolting from Cindy, he was running from the one who could save him. Fortunately, Cindy saw his need, and she had the experience and skill to safely capture him in spite of himself.

The same was true of the man who caught the wild hawk whipping through my greenhouse.

I first saw the bird on a Sunday afternoon. I had climbed to the top of my property, where I have a wood and mesh enclosure for fruit trees and orchids. This greenhouse keeps the squirrels from eating my apples and apricots, and lets me hang suitable orchids outdoors where they can get misted on a timer. I saw a whooshing movement and realized that a bird was trapped inside. Likely a gardener had been working there and not noticed the bird slip in.

After consulting a neighbor, I felt fairly certain that my "prisoner" was a hawk. The hawk was flying with such force that I didn't feel safe stepping in to try to guide it. On the advice of animal control, I opened the door wide and hoped the hawk would fly out overnight.

Morning came and the bird was still whooshing around, unaware it could leave.

It so happened I was in the middle of a house remodel. I asked my workmen about the hawk. They agreed that it would probably not be safe to approach the bird, and another call to animal control was in order. Then one of them recalled that my painter, Gerardo, knew about such things. Maybe he could help. Gerardo arrived, and before I could blink he'd gone up to the greenhouse, caught the hawk with his bare hands, and released it to freedom.

I was stunned. Clearly catching a hawk barehanded would have been a terribly dangerous thing for most people to do. But Gerardo had the experience and skill. In a different way than Cindy, he captured that bird to set it free, and did for the hawk what it couldn't do for itself.

God has done for me what I couldn't do for myself—captured me to set me free from sin and death.

Like Frost, I was sitting out in the cold of a life without Jesus, my Messiah. Like that furry orphan, I was hungry—starved for God's unconditional love. Like the hawk, I was swooping back and forth in my cage, unable to fly through the door of God's forgiveness on my own. But also like Frost and the hawk, I had a skilled catcher who knew just how to capture me—God's Holy Spirit. He drew me close through the love of some Christians on my college campus, and coaxed me into His kingdom with Old Testament prophecy. Like Frost, I was leery even after I entered in, but He continued to care for me and grow my trust in Him, and now the last thing I would ever want to do is flee His loving embrace.

No one understood better than the apostle Paul that God catches us to free us. In Romans 6:22-23 he wrote, "But now that you have been set free from sin and have become slaves to God, the benefit you reap leads to holiness, and the result is eternal life. For the wages of sin is death, but the gift of God is eternal life in Christ Jesus our Lord."

Frost is safe and flourishing because a human cared enough to become a "catcher of cats." God wants His children to be "fishers of people." He wants our hearts to go out to those wandering in the spiritual cold, where Satan prowls. If we will allow God's Spirit to work through us, we can be the arms and legs of His love to draw frightened strays into His eternal home.

"Come, follow me," Jesus said, "and I will send you out to fish for people" (Matthew 4:19).

Consider This:

How did God draw you into His kingdom? Is there a particular person or persons He used to help "catch" you? Can you point to specific areas where you've been set free? Is there someone in your life right now who is spiritually wandering in the cold? How might God use you to coax them to safety?

Gerti Goes to the Gophers
Follow God's Call

*A ship is safe in harbor, but that's
not what ships are for.*

WILLIAM SHEDD

Gerti and Rosie both belonged to Debbie Enns and her family. They were female black and white kitties and looked a lot alike. But there was one important difference. Rosie got there first.

Rosie came from one of our litters. Gerti and a tabby named Gus came from one of Debbie's students. They needed a place to grow up, so Debbie took them in. Rosie already viewed the Enns' home as her domain, to rule as she saw fit. It seemed like Gerti didn't quite agree, but she seemed to sense that if she fought Rosie, she would lose.

Maybe Gerti got tired of the tension. Maybe she decided the Enns family wasn't to be her appointed place. Maybe she started checking out the other homes around them. However it happened, she found a "calling" that caused her to venture forth.

There was a neighbor across the street who had a big problem. She had gophers everywhere. Gopher mounds covered her front yard. Gerti discovered the gophers. She found the gopher hunt to be fabulous entertainment. The neighbor was delighted and rewarded Gerti with special food. She and her children became Gerti's new family. Gerti loved being appreciated and honored as a conqueror. She loved being the ruling cat in her new home, rather than being treated as an intruder. The neighbor didn't know Gerti had a family already, and decided to adopt her. She changed Gerti's name to Gophia the gopher chaser.

Before too long, Gerti/Gophia decided to go back and visit her old family. Debbie welcomed her with open arms. She petted Gerti and fed her special treats. But Rosie seemed less pleased that the "intruder" was back. Soon Gerti crossed the street again to the neighbor's, where she was hailed as a hero.

Then one day, Debbie noticed how much better her neighbor's once gopher-infested yard was looking. She asked her neighbor what treatment she was using. Just about that time, Gerti showed up. Debbie greeted her with a "Hi, Gerti! Whatcha been up to, girl?" The neighbor giggled. "She's been chasing gophers. This is my fabulous new gopher treatment—Gophia!"

Debbie and her neighbor had a good laugh. They shared stories about Gerti/Gophia, and agreed to share the cat too.

Gerti/Gophia got me thinking. She left her home to "serve" somewhere else, and received a new name that reflected her new purpose. In a much more intentional way, we are often called by God to leave home in order to fulfill His purpose for us.

After college graduation, our daughter, Karen, prayed about where God would want her to work and live. She moved back to her old hometown of Bakersfield and tried a few jobs. But she wasn't finding fulfillment. She decided to apply for work at Disneyland.

Karen was hired in guest relations, the job she wanted most. She felt a bit anxious about leaving home. But she loves working at Disneyland and has found new purpose. She gets to serve people in many different ways. She gives VIP tours of the park for movie stars, athletes, and other celebrities from all over the world. But she also guides a wide range of other people who have come to have fun at Disneyland. She enjoys telling them all about Walt Disney and making them feel comfortable throughout the day. She is also part of a program at Disneyland called YES (Youth Education Series), for which she teaches classes to students.

There are times when Karen wishes she lived closer to home. But being where God has placed her trumps all that. She even has a new "extra name" that reflects what she does—"cast member." She is thrilled to be part of the Disney magic. She takes wonderful pleasure in watching small children's eyes brighten when she helps their dreams come true. Just the other day, she got to introduce a little girl from Slovakia to Donald Duck and watch them hold hands as they walked down the street together.

I truly believe that Karen has found her calling at Disneyland. She loves people. They see the joy in her heart and like to be around her. And even though there are things she may not be able to share on a secular job, I know those around her are seeing the Lord shine through her.

Gerti/Gophia enjoys going home to the Enns' and loves to be loved there. Then she returns to the neighbors where she feels called to be. She is happy there as well because she is doing what she senses she is supposed to do.

Karen loves to come home, be with her family, relax, and be loved. But when it's time to return to work, she goes happily, because she knows it is where God has sent her.

The apostle Paul was originally a Pharisee named Saul. Then Jesus called Saul to follow Him—and not only share the gospel with Jews, but become the apostle to the Gentiles. Saul became Paul. God called him forth from the church at Antioch to go on several missionary journeys. Paul endured tremendous hardships, but the joy of fulfilling God's purpose for him trumped them all. Though he returned periodically to his home church, he always went out again in answer to God's call on his life.

Like Gophia, Karen, and Paul, we have a purpose to fulfill. Are you willing to seek and obey God's call on your life, even if it means leaving home like they did? If so, He will be with you and bless you, no matter what hardships may come, as you trust and follow Him.

While they were worshiping the Lord and fasting, the Holy Spirit said, "Set apart for me Barnabas and Saul for the work to which I have called them." So after they had fasted and prayed, they placed their hands on them and sent them off (Acts 13:2-3).

Consider This:

Has God ever encouraged you to leave home to fulfill His purpose for you? What most frightened you about this call? What most excited you? Did you obey? What happened? If you refused the call then, have you prayed and asked God if there might be a call on your life now that He wants you to pursue?

Cat Wars
Conflicts Have Unintended Casualties

*Peace is costly but it
is worth the expense.*

AFRICAN PROVERB

Some years ago, a friend who knew my kitties well told me Muffin wanted to be an only cat. At the time, Muffin had three kitty house-mates—two seniors and a big orange tabby named Merlin. I'd got-ten Merlin to be her pal, but they didn't quite hit it off. She alternated between grudging coexistence and outraged shrieks when he pounced on her. I think he was just trying to play, but he was a bit too rough for my little "princess with paws." Still, I was not to be deterred. When I lost Merlin to cancer, I welcomed a one-year-old male flame point Ragdoll kitty named Bo to be Muffin's new buddy.

Muffin wasn't thrilled with this new brother either, but I was deter-mined to convince her. I am still convincing, though it's going better. But there are moments when it's "cat wars"—mostly due to jealousy over me. Normally there are no lasting consequences, but one day their conflict had an unintended victim.

My friend Ashley and her family had joined me for dinner that night. We were gathered around the den TV, eating on trays. I was on the couch, with the cats on one side and Ashley on the other. Suddenly Muffin and Bo got into it. I heard an angry screech, and the cats flew across the couch past me and Ashley, badly scratching her arm in the process.

Ashley treated the wound with antibiotic ointment, and fortunately it didn't get infected. But it ached for the rest of the evening. My cats didn't mean to injure my friend, but they did. This guest human was in the path of their wrath and got hurt. My cats had no way to anticipate or control the unintended fallout from their spat.

Human conflict has unintended victims too. Some months later, I did just what Muffin and Bo had. I screeched and lunged and caused harm I never meant to inflict.

I was in the midst of a house remodel. I'd been living in the middle of the mess, along with my kitties and puppies. Some days, it seemed like workmen were everywhere. On this morning, I felt like I had nowhere to be. My frustration and stress spilled over, and I spewed my irritation in the presence of my painter and wallpaper hanger. They were trying to figure out where they and their helpers would work for the day. After I left, Gerardo the painter joked to his colleague, "Do you want to be everywhere?" Thanks to the tone I'd set, Gerardo's colleague apparently didn't see the intended humor in that statement.

I didn't realize the effect I'd had. But a lovely Christian friend was helping to oversee the project. She came to me and shared what had happened. She said things now seemed tense between them and my words and mood had triggered the problem. I felt awful that I had strained the relationship between these two workers who had just been trying to do their jobs and please me. I thought back to how Muffin and Bo had scratched Ashley. Knowing that my painter loved four-foots, I saw a way to hopefully put some ointment on this emotional wound and bring healing.

I told Gerardo the story of how Bo and Muffin had scratched Ashley. Then I shared that I felt I'd done something similar. By getting out of sorts in their presence, I'd set the wrong tone and triggered the tension between him and his colleague. I apologized for "scratching" their relationship and asked if he would talk with his coworker. He chuckled at my cat story, did as I asked, and things were smoothed over.

Many centuries ago, an innocent party was terribly wounded by a conflict over Israel's throne. God had anointed Saul to be Israel's first king. But Saul had done things that caused God to revoke that kingship. Through the prophet Samuel, God chose David to be Saul's successor.

Saul did not go quietly, though. He soon guessed that the young shepherd-boy-turned-warrior who slew the Philistine giant Goliath was God's likely pick. Even while David was in Saul's service, Saul tried to kill him. Caught in the middle was Saul's son Jonathan, who was David's dear friend.

At first, Jonathan didn't believe his father really meant David harm. But when he tested his father, he learned otherwise. Saul exploded, saying, "You son of a perverse and rebellious woman! Don't I know that you have sided with the son of Jesse to your own shame and to the shame of the mother who bore you? As long as the son of Jesse lives on this earth, neither you nor your kingdom will be established. Now send someone to bring him to me, for he must die!" (1 Samuel 20:30-31)

Saul's real quarrel was with David, but his own son Jonathan was caught in the crossfire. Jonathan stayed loyal to David, but one can only guess at the pain and grief this situation caused him. In the end, Jonathan and two of his brothers were killed in a battle with the Philistines, his father fell on his own sword rather than be captured, and David went on to ascend the throne just as God had decreed.

Muffin and Bo don't understand how their conflicts may impact others. We humans do, and we can consider the cost. We can seek and pursue peace, and work for healing and restoration when unintended wounds occur. By doing so, we will follow Jesus, our Prince of Peace, who said, "Blessed are the peacemakers: for they shall be called the children of God" (Matthew 5:9 KJV).

Make every effort to keep the unity of the Spirit through the bond of peace (Ephesians 4:3).

Consider This:

Have you ever been in a conflict that caused unintended harm? What happened? How did it impact people's lives? Was any effort made to bring healing and restoration? If so, did it help? If not, would God want you to reach out now?

Spooky KO'd

Stop and Smell the Blessings

He that can take rest is greater
than he that can take cities.

BENJAMIN FRANKLIN

When my husband Steve was a little boy, he and his sister Chrissy had a cat that spiced their family's life with lots of comedy and drama. Spooky was dark gray and orange and a perpetual motion machine. She loved playing with the children's toys, pushing them around with her furry little paws. When Steve had spent hours building and creating with his Lincoln Logs, Spooky would delight to escape with a log Steve knew would be the final touch on his masterpiece. When Chrissy played with her Barbie dolls and had everything arranged just the way she liked it, Spooky would plow through all the clothes, messing up the house or store that Chrissy had so carefully designed.

Usually, Steve and Chrissy reacted good-humoredly to Spooky's antics. They'd yell playfully and chase her through the house until their mom stopped them and settled them down. Many times Spooky wouldn't stay settled down, though. She'd take off again, jumping on and off the furniture and racing up and down the curtains in a way Steve's mom found quite upsetting. All this made Steve and Chrissy laugh until they cried.

One day Spooky was doing her perpetual motion thing when she went a little too far. There was a program on TV and she stopped her antics to "watch" it. Suddenly she leaped at the screen as if to jump right into the picture. This mighty endeavor knocked her out. For a short while, she lay there KO'd. Fortunately, before long she leaped up and continued her run. She never learned to slow down, but her family loved her dearly anyway.

Spooky's behavior reminds me of how I can be when I try to do too much. I run from one project to another, staying in perpetual motion but not always accomplishing what really matters. I hurl myself at my schedule, not knowing I'm about to get knocked out. On one particular day, my husband had to step in. I told Steve all I'd planned to do—go to the market, work on a church project, visit a sick friend, go to the doctor, look for some new shoes. He stopped me in my tracks and helped me see how ridiculous I was being. He called a halt before I hit the wall and got KO'd, as Spooky had.

Other times, God has chosen to stop me. When the children were little, I helped produce the annual Christmas program at their school. It was a tremendous amount of work, but I loved it. After all the weeks of work were done and the program was over, everyone was happy and it was time for Christmas vacation. But that didn't mean I stopped running. Now it was time to decorate for Christmas and enjoy all of the festivities. One year our extended family met at the beach. I had a bad cold but never took time to take care of it. After everyone went home, I wound up in the hospital with pneumonia. I got discouraged and called my mom. She comforted me with something she'd read. Mom applied the quote to me. She said, "Connie, God didn't call you into illness. He called you into stillness."

If we ask God to plan our steps and try to be obedient to Him, we will get things done and not get knocked out. I recall another time when I had a long list of errands to run. My first stop was the bank. On my way back to the car, I saw a good friend I hadn't spoken with in a long while. I asked her to join me in my car and we sat and visited for quite some time. We caught up on our lives and families. We took time to "stop and smell the blessings," and God blessed us for doing so. We both had busy lives, but because we took this time, we both felt revived and renewed. All the rest of my errands waited till the next day. Every-thing still got done, just a little later, and that was fine.

The memory of a sweet conversation with a good friend has contin-ued to be a blessing. And it has taught me to slow down occasionally and take time to wait on the Lord.

No one knows our need for rest better than the God who made us. He not only wants us to rest, He commands it. One of His Ten Com-mandments is to keep the Sabbath He ordained. In Exodus 20:8-11 God says, "Remember the Sabbath day by keeping it holy. Six days you shall labor and do all your work, but the seventh day is a Sabbath to the LORD your God. On it you shall not do any work, neither you, nor your son or daughter, nor your male or female servant, nor your animals, nor the for-eigner residing in your towns. For in six days the LORD made the heavens and the earth, the sea, and all that is in them, but he rested on the sev-enth day. Therefore the LORD blessed the Sabbath day and made it holy."

God gave us the Sabbath as a time to rest, smell the blessings, and be with Him. It is a time to stop running so we don't get KO'd, like Spooky did all those years ago. He created us, He knows what we need, and we will be healthier in every way if we rest, and rest in Him.

Then Jesus said, "Come to me, all of you who are weary and carry heavy burdens, and I will give you rest" (Mat-thew 11:28, NLT).

Consider This:

Is your life a perpetual motion machine, like Spooky's? If so, what effect has this had on your health? Your family? Your walk with the Lord? Have you recently stopped to smell the blessings? What benefits resulted? Do you set aside a day each week as a Sabbath to rest and spend time with the Lord? If not, will you pray about doing so?

Hiding under the Covers
Keep On Keeping On

To be lost in spiritlessness is the
most terrible thing of all.

SØREN KIERKEGAARD

Mooch hadn't felt well the night before. We knew that because our nine-year-old cat had left some of his dinner on the hallway floor. After cleaning up the mess I glanced around, but didn't see him. He didn't show up for breakfast the next morning, either. I searched the house and yard, but he was nowhere to be found. My husband even checked his office, since lately Mooch had taken to sleeping there. Still nothing. I was really worried by now. My family figured he was just hiding away somewhere to sleep off whatever ailed him. But as I left to run errands, I urged them to call me as soon as Mooch was spotted.

Within two hours, my husband phoned with the good news that he'd had a Mooch sighting. Mooch had indeed been hiding in Phil's office. A soft, scratching sound got Phil's attention, and he looked over just in time to see Mooch's head appear, followed by a very flattened body as he wriggled his way out from under the computer desk. Mooch stretched and looked up at Phil expectantly for a touch. He was just fine! It had been just as my family guessed; Mooch had been a bit under the weather and needed to sleep it off.

My precious daughter-in-law, Andrea, went through a period when she wished she could sleep off her troubles. She and our son had been having financial problems. The city where they lived got slammed by the economic downturn in 2008. Though our son pastored a church, he paid bills by working in construction. Projects shut down, leaving all new housing tracts unfinished. Prior to this, the place had been booming and people were flocking to what was considered a top new area to live. Now work was horribly scarce. Andrea was a stay-at-home mom with three young children. Making ends meet became a losing battle. It was so stressful Andrea wished she could climb into bed, hide under the covers and sleep off the crisis—just as Mooch slept off his misery.

Instead, however, she fought to keep herself above the feelings that threatened to drag her down. Each new day she intentionally counted her blessings and put her trust in God. She told me she never thought she'd need help from her Christian community to make it—but she did. Since we too had been set back by the country's recession and had needed help, I empathized completely. We both hoped someday to be in the position to give rather than to receive, and we promised each other not to take to "sleeping it off" as Mooch had.

There was a time when the prophet Elijah felt the same way. He had successfully confronted the prophets of Baal. This did not please King Ahab's wife, Jezebel, and she threatened to kill him. His response was to run. He fled into the desert alone, sat under a tree, and begged God to die. "'I have had enough, Lord,' he said. 'Take my life; I am no better than my ancestors'" (1 Kings 19:4). Then he lay down and tried to "sleep it off," but God had other plans. He sent an angel to feed and strengthen Elijah so he could travel to Mount Horeb. There he heard God's voice as a gentle whisper and learned his situation wasn't as desperate as he had thought.

Mooch is a cat. He's allowed to sleep off what gets him down. But we humans can't do that, at least not whenever we feel like it, because we need to be there for our loved ones. So, what can we do when our troubles make us want to bury our heads? We can count our blessings, trust and praise the Lord, and keep on keeping on. That's what Andrea did, and that's what Elijah learned to do. So, the next time you feel like pulling the covers over your head and emulating Mooch by sleeping until things get better, remember that God is not the author of discouragement. It is the enemy who wants us to give up. Our God is a faithful God who will help us walk on our troubled waters if we keep our eyes on Him.

Why, my soul, are you downcast? Why so disturbed within me? Put your hope in God, for I will yet praise him, my Savior and my God (Psalm 42:5).

Consider This:

Are you going through something right now that makes you want to climb in bed and pull the covers over your head? Can you list your blessings and thank God for what you do have instead? Would you also praise Him for His marvelous attributes which remind us that whatever our problems, He is greater?

A Little Cat Shall Lead Them

Are You Eager to Give?

*The manner of giving is worth
more than the gift.*

PIERRE CORNEILLE

Cats love to bring "offerings" to their masters. Such gifts are often dead birds, rodents, or bugs. Leia was an indoor kitty and didn't have access to any live prey, so she got creative and chose small, inanimate objects to present for her people's approval.

Leia's humans always knew when she had a gift for them. They'd hear a strange meow—strange because the cat was mewing with her mouth full. She'd trot over, drop her offering at their feet, and wait for it to be noticed and acknowledged with a "good kitty."

One night late, when Leia's masters were in bed, they heard a thumping and mewing. Leia was literally throwing herself against the door to their bedroom. When they opened it, she trotted in with a small bean-bag animal in her mouth and laid it before them. She had been so passionate and desperate to give her latest gift that she had literally been trying to pound the door open with her little body.

Leia's people are in the entertainment industry. Recently, they let a friend use their home for a video shoot. The cats were confined all day and released when the shoot was over. Leia's people heard her pacing the halls and mewing all night. Next morning, their young daughter had a beanbag with a smiley face waiting at her bedroom door, and they had a plastic doo-dad at theirs. Clearly Leia had been "gifting" yet again.

What grabs my heart about Leia's gifting is her passionate eagerness to do so. A little boy named Owen shows the same passionate delight in giving food gift cards to the homeless.

Eight-year-old Owen and his family live in a small town in Oregon where his father pastors a church. Owen loves the Lord, and understands that it pleases God when His children give—especially to those less fortunate than themselves. He knows giving to "the least of these" is also an offering to the Lord. One of the ways Owen's family does this is to buy five-dollar gift cards to a local fast food restaurant and keep them in the car to give to homeless people they may encounter.

Owen's mom is very careful to keep him safe. She is discerning about people and if she senses anything amiss, she doesn't let Owen proceed. She has also taught all her children that they must never approach or talk to strangers on their own. But when they are with their parents, Owen, his brother Everett, and his sister Eleni are allowed to participate in the giving of these gift cards under very carefully controlled circumstances.

There is a particular area of town where homeless people tend to congregate. When his mom drives past this area, Owen watches eagerly from his spot buckled into the back seat of the family car. He will call out to his mom if he sees someone who might benefit from a gift card. For Owen to safely give, the car must be stopped at a red light so he can undo his seat belt, grab a gift card, roll down the window, offer his gift, and belt himself in again. That means his mom may need to circle the block once or twice so the timing works out. But he is insistent and eager and passionate—just like Leia the cat—and his mom does her best to fulfill this child's (and his siblings') desire to give their gift and know the joy of helping others.

As I think of Owen and Leia, it seems that this child and this cat have something marvelous in common. They give with a joyous and eager abandon. They make me think of Paul's words to the Corinthians (2 Corinthians 9:7): "Each of you should give what you have decided in your heart to give, not reluctantly or under compulsion, for God loves a cheerful giver." My coauthor Dottie, a Bible teacher, tells me the word "cheerful" might also be translated "without grudging." In other words, God wants us to have the same joy and eagerness in our gifting that Leia and Owen do.

If I am honest, I must admit that I don't always give with their heart of joy. I have even asked myself if I gave more easily when I had less, and am sometimes a bit more reluctant now that I have more. Sure, I understand that everything I am and have is really God's. I sincerely pray for His guidance in the area of stewardship and seek His direction, and His wisdom. I have seen Him very specifically lead me about where to give, and how much. But do I have the eager, unrestrained passion to give that this cat and child do? And am I willing to give not just of my "stuff," but of my time, and talents, and love? If truth be told, when it comes to heart attitude, this little child and cat could lead me…and do.

Jesus once compared a widow's tiny monetary gift to God with that of far wealthier folks. He said the widow's gift was greater because she had given all she had. Jesus also gave all He had—He gave His life for me. If my heart is to give all I am and have to Him, and obey His leading as He uses me to bless others, I will share in His joy.

He also saw a poor widow put in two very small copper coins. "Truly I tell you," he said, "this poor widow has put in more than all the others. All these people gave their gifts out of their wealth; but she out of her poverty put in all she had to live on" (Luke 21:2-4).

Consider This:

What is the most joyful giving experience you have ever had? What made it so special? Is there an area of your life where you struggle to give? Why do you think that is so? Will you pray and ask God to change your heart?

Bo Slays His Giants
Enter into God's Promises

A smooth sea never made a skilled mariner.

ENGLISH PROVERB

Bo was just under a year old when I "called" him to leave his people in Texas and join me in the promised land of Los Angeles. He was the last kitten left from a litter of four. I found out about him online, and when I saw this beautiful flame point Ragdoll's photo, I fell in love.

Like the Israelites of old, Bo had some desert to cross before he reached "Canaan." Someone skilled in transporting cats drove him out by car, and he did great. But he also had a few "giants" to slay before he could dwell in peace and safety in his new life with me. He would have to win acceptance from my three other kitties, whose first instinctive territorial response would doubtless be hissing and spitting. I'd dealt with this process before, and I knew how to help him through it. He would also have to figure out that my dogs were harmless, friendly critters—much more friendly than the cats if truth be told. These "giants" didn't seem all that big, and I knew he'd prevail with my aid.

Little did I dream that a much bigger giant was looming for us both—a giant that would shake my world to its foundations. Just days after Bo's arrival, my 90-year-old mother had a massive heart attack.

103

Mom lived an hour and a half away and I needed to rush to her side literally at a moment's notice. I could take the dogs but I'd need to leave the cats, and I'd have to isolate Bo from the others.

I made a frantic call to friends who'd helped out with cat feeding in the past. They agreed to pitch in for as long as was needed. I left Bo in a large bathroom with food, water, and a litter box, and sped onto the freeway, not even sure Mom would still be alive when I reached her.

Mom survived, but I was gone for the better part of two weeks. During that time, Bo proved his giant-slaying mettle. He took "kitty isolation" in stride. He won the heart of my friends' young daughter, who petted and played with him and pronounced him a fabulous cat. And once I was able to spend a bit more time at home again, he quickly overcame his fear of my dogs and found his place in the kitty pecking order. With my help, he'd overcome his obstacles and could start entering into the wonderful blessings of his new home.

A young boy named Owen recently embarked on a journey similar to Bo's. He and his family moved to the "promised land" of Scotland. His dad was following God's call to get a doctorate in theology and teach at the college level. God had done some marvelous miracles to confirm the family's path. But it meant Owen had some giants to slay—giants that seemed pretty big to an eight-year-old.

One of those giants was making new friends. Owen was leaving such a close pal behind, he wasn't sure he'd ever have another buddy like him. Owen's parents prayed God would give him a new friend right away. God did. The family that was waiting to greet them when they arrived at their rental house in Scotland had a little boy just Owen's age. He and Owen are becoming pals and Owen even got invited to this boy's birthday party.

Another giant Owen had to overcome was language comprehension. English is spoken in Scotland, but it sounds a lot different. School personnel warned Owen's parents that he and his younger brother and sister would have trouble with the accent. They took the school's advice and arrived a few weeks before the start of class to give the kids time to adjust. Owen's mom, Andrea, asked the kids to tell her the minute they started understanding what people were saying.

That giant-slaying answer to prayer snuck up on Andrea unexpectedly. Owen tugged her arm while she was speaking with someone. Her first instinct was to be annoyed because he was interrupting her. Then he said, "Mom, I understand." He had had his language breakthrough.

Owen and his family couldn't have slain these and other giants on their own. They chose to follow God's call and leave giants to Him. God asked the Israelites of old to make a similar choice. They balked at first and spent 40 years wandering in the wilderness until a new generation took the doubters' place. God then used Joshua to lead them into Canaan and gave them the land, as He'd promised.

In this life, no "promised land" is problem-free. Bo has spats with my other Ragdoll kitty, Muffin. Owen and his family will face more challenges during their stay in Scotland. And all of us will be tempted to cower at the size of the "giants" in our path instead of gazing at the bigness of God when He calls us to go beyond our comfort levels on this journey called life. But there is no other path to the fullness of God's promises, and He has promised to walk it with us and clear it for us if we will trust, obey, and put our hand in His.

Be strong and courageous, because you will lead these people to inherit the land I swore to their ancestors to give them (Joshua 1:6).

Consider This:

Is God calling you to follow Him to some new "promised land"? What "giants" are looming before you? Are you willing to trust the Lord and move forward? What biblical promises might encourage you?

Tiny Lioness
Be a "Square Peg" for God

One who walks in another's
tracks leaves no footprints.

<small>PROVERB</small>

When I went to pick up my young friend Stephanie for lunch, I was expecting to mentor her. Instead, her tiny kitten mentored me.

Missy was a little Siamese, about four months old. She was the only kitten in a home with seven adult dogs and 11 new puppies. But if she was "odd kitten out," she didn't seem to notice. She was self-assured and perfectly happy to be part of the group. She stepped cautiously among the dogs, peering at the puppies but being careful not to disturb them. She seemed so calm and collected, I wondered if perhaps she thought she was a dog too. I imagined her loving the dogs as her family, and them accepting her as one of their own.

Missy gave me food for thought all that day—and I'm thinking still. She was smaller than even the tiniest Chihuahua in her home. Yet she was poised and confident, like a tiny, proud lioness walking about her kingdom.

There have been times in my life when, like Missy, I was "odd kitten out." But instead of being poised and confident, I felt lost and out of place when surrounded with those who seemed different from me. One such time was when my husband and I decided that I would go back to college. I planned to get a teaching credential so I could work and help finance our children's college education.

Just about all of the other students were teenagers or young adults in their twenties. I started out feeling like a square peg in a round hole. But I realized God put me there for a reason. I resolved to walk with courage. Over time, most of the young people in my classes became my friends. They would talk to me about their problems and I would listen and pray. I was discovering that what was different about me could bless those around me.

Then I took a class whose professor seemed to send a mixed message. He urged his students to think for themselves, but we all felt unspoken pressure to agree with everything our teacher said. I decided not to give in. When I was invited to express my opinion, I spoke up politely and shared my true beliefs. Several others in the class came up to me later. They said they couldn't speak their minds and hearts, but they would pray for me to continue to have the courage to do so. They helped me bloom where I was planted and put my confidence in God so I could be a square peg for Him.

Many centuries ago, a biblical character named Joseph also found himself "odd person out." He was sold into slavery by his own brothers and carried off to Egypt to be a slave. But instead of feeling out of place, he trusted God and bloomed everywhere he was planted—even in prison. He stayed true to God's moral standards, did his work with excellence, and looked to God to use him to interpret others' dreams. Because Joseph was willing to be a square peg for God, he became a ruler in Egypt, second only to Pharaoh himself. Joseph also became the instrument by which God saved the Hebrews from famine and preserved them for His purposes. Joseph himself recognized this, telling his brothers, "And now, do not be distressed and do not be angry with yourselves for selling me here, because it was to save lives that God sent me ahead of you" (Genesis 45:5).

Just as Missy was called to be the lone kitten in a household of dogs, we may be called to be the lone believer in a particular situation. If we depend on our outward circumstances for our confidence and try to be like those around us, we are apt to feel self-conscious and "odd person out." But, if we look to God for our confidence and sense of belonging, we can be bold and brave to love those who are different than we are and serve God's purposes.

It's not the look of a lion but the heart of a lion that counts!

For the LORD will be at your side and will keep your foot from being snared (Proverbs 3:26).

Consider This:

Has God ever called you to be a square peg in a round hole for Him? What did you find hardest about your situation? How did you respond? What were the results? What did you learn that might help you encourage someone else God has called to be "odd person out?"

Allergic to Life

How's Your Spiritual Immune System?

*If you are allergic to a thing, it is best
not to put that thing in your mouth,
particularly if the thing is cats.*

LEMONY SNICKET

I refer to my boy cat, Bo, as my giant "plush toy." He has gorgeous cream fur accented with orange. At over 13 pounds, he outweighs all my other four-foots, even my dogs. For most of his four years, he has been the picture of health. But there was one notable exception, and it nearly killed him.

I had taken Bo to the vet for an immunization. He had a slight health blip and we considered postponing the shot, but decided it would be okay to give it. I brought Bo home, expecting him to be fine. He wasn't. Over the course of that day, he started acting sicker and sicker. By the next morning I knew something was drastically wrong. I rushed Bo back to my vet during pre-office hours "drop-off time" and urged that he be seen immediately. The receptionists told me to leave him and promised he'd be checked right away.

My vet called an hour later. He said it was a very good thing I'd brought Bo in when I had. Bo had a 106-degree fever. If I had waited any longer, he might have suffered brain damage or died.

At the time, we weren't quite sure what had made Bo so sick. I, of course, wondered if that little blip had been a warning sign. But Bo's vet told me he suspected "fever of unknown origin." Some cats, for whatever reason, suddenly spike a very high temperature. Bo's doctor told me that though the cause was unknown, vets knew how to treat this, and Bo's recovery prospects were excellent. And usually once this happened, it didn't recur. There was also a chance that Bo had had an allergic reaction to his immunization. Just in case that might be the culprit, we would wait an extra length of time before considering giving him a booster.

Happily, the vet's prognosis was correct. Bo recovered fully from his crisis. When the time came for him to have this particular booster, I delayed it. Then, when he was in for a checkup, I asked Bo's doctor about the matter. He looked back at Bo's records, and now felt the odds were high that Bo's illness had indeed been an allergic reaction. The very shot that was supposed to help protect Bo's life had likely threatened it instead. Bo's vet asked me if my cat ever went outside. When I said no, he told me there was no reason to *ever* risk giving him that vaccination again.

Bo is not the only special bundle of joy in my world who almost died from something that normally promotes health and life. My friend's toddler, Darla, is a highly allergic child. This little girl once broke out in welts simply from *touching* dairy. She is allergic to a host of foods, and has twice had reactions that have sent her and her parents to the emergency room. Darla's mom and dad don't dare take her to a restaurant. When they visit someone else's home, they must be sure Darla can't come in contact with even crumbs of the items she's sensitive to. They are working with an allergist, and they hope that in time she can be desensitized to some of the foods that threaten her. But unless there's a medical breakthrough, there are certain ones she may need to avoid for the rest of her days.

In the case of both Bo and Darla, their immune systems are out of whack. Things that are meant to give life threaten life. Their situations got me thinking about how, in a whole different way, we humans can be "allergic" to what gives life spiritually.

I am a Jewish believer in Jesus. I was fortunate not to have had any negative experiences with those who called themselves Christians. But historically, there has been persecution of Jews and forced conversion of Jews by some who wore the Christian label. They may not have truly had a personal relationship with God or behaved as Jesus urges His followers to act. Or in some cases, they may not have understood what it really means to follow Jesus. Regardless, their behavior has set the stage for allergic reactions to Christianity and the gospel message among at least some in the Jewish community.

Jews are not the only ones who may become sensitized to the gospel because of others' behavior. It can happen to anybody. I knew someone whose "allergy" stemmed from the actions of a relative. This relative pushed his beliefs on others while treating his own family in a way that seemed very much at odds with his professed faith. A whole host of negative experiences with individuals, groups, or churches can prime someone to respond to the gospel and those who would share it by breaking out in "spiritual hives" or running the other way.

Bo can live a long, happy life without getting the shot that threatens his well-being. Darla can grow strong and healthy while avoiding her food triggers, though it's harder. But the Bible says that to have eternal life, we must put our faith in the sacrifice our Messiah made to wipe our sins away forever. So, how can we "desensitize" those whose allergic reactions may hinder them from hearing this life-giving message?

I talked about this with a dear friend who has decades of experience in ministry. We agreed that the power of God's love flowing through His people is huge. Loving others with no strings attached, letting them get to know us without forcing a discussion about our faith prematurely, can make an enormous difference.

My friend's ministry staff has learned the power of this unconditional love. In one instance, they had a chance to take a group of elderly Jewish immigrants on a couple of outings. They enjoyed each other and began to form a bond of friendship. Life was hard for these elderly folks, and the ministry staff felt a tug on their hearts to make things easier for their new friends. They began visiting on a regular basis. They brought canned goods and other useful items, and expressed their love by simply spending time with this wonderful group of older people.

They didn't make their beliefs a secret, but they didn't push them either. After a while, these seniors asked their ministry friends to start a Bible study with them.

The apostle Paul, a leading first century messenger of the gospel, recognized the crucial importance of love. That's why he wrote to the Ephesians, "Follow God's example, therefore, as dearly loved children and walk in the way of love, just as Christ loved us and gave himself up for us as a fragrant offering and sacrifice to God" (Ephesians 5:1-2).

I don't know if Bo's or Darla's physical immune systems can fully heal. But I know God wants to heal us all spiritually. If, instead of sensitizing others, we stay sensitive to them and God's Spirit, we can be God's instruments to draw them to life-giving faith in Him.

But during the night an angel of the Lord opened the doors of the jail and brought them (the apostles) out. "Go, stand in the temple courts," he said, "and tell the people all about this new life" (Acts 5:19-20).

Consider This:

Do you know anyone who is "allergic" to the gospel message? Is there a way you could simply reach out to them in friendship? Have you ever behaved in a way that needlessly turned someone off to your faith? Is there a way you could make amends?

The Copycat Blues
Watch Out What Rubs Off

Bad habits are like a comfortable bed,
easy to get into, but hard to get out of.

ANONYMOUS

Monte was a teenaged friend of our family who spent a lot of fun time with our son John and worked with our daughter Karen on our farm in the summer. One year he picked out a kitten from a litter we had. He chose this particular kitty because it had a big head and swaggered when it walked. He named it Arnold because it reminded him of a teacher from his youth.

When Arnold was old enough, Monte took him home to join his new human family—a mom and dad and two teenaged boys. Arnold soon felt welcomed and loved and found his own special places on the sofa, on Monte's bed, and outside in their yard. Arnold also began to pick up the habits of his new family and learn how to survive in a teenaged world.

As loving as this family was, Monte and his brother also liked to tease. This behavior quickly rubbed off on Arnold. He would often sit on the back of the sofa and reach out his paw to swipe people as they walked by. If he did it to one of the boys, he'd get playfully thrown to the floor and tackled. Arnold would hold his own as they rolled across the carpet. He learned how to return the tackle with an attack of his own. Though he was large for a cat, Arnold was of course much smaller than any of his human family. He could easily have been hurt trying to keep up with the boys. They realized this and were careful with him. When the playing was done, Arnold joined the guys on the floor as they watched television or read a book. Though Arnold's teasing could have been a bad habit that put him at risk, his loving family made sure it remained harmless fun.

Arnold also learned some good habits from his new family. Monte's parents, Glen and Susie, loved having people come over. When guests arrived, Arnold jumped up and greeted them at the door, right along with the humans of the home. Glen and Susie were also active in the neighborhood, helping others and joining in on community events. Arnold would come along and observe as if he were the executive producer. Arnold grew into a strong, independent cat with royal-like qualities and an outgoing, friendly attitude. Everyone in the neighborhood knew him and loved him. He would walk down the sidewalk and people would greet him with a happy, "Hi Arnold! How ya doin'?" Love and friendliness were good habits that served Arnold well and blessed others.

I have also had good and bad habits rub off on me in my life. Though I am over 50 years old, I still remember how I behaved in junior high. Like Arnold, I had friends who teased, and I mimicked their behavior. But my teasing became hurtful. I recall walking home behind a boy I liked and saying terrible things to him all the way, making fun of his clothes and his walk. Actually, I liked him and I was trying to get a response out of him. But I'm sure I hurt his feelings. I didn't like myself very much, and I think I made it hard for others to like me too.

In high school I rededicated my life to God. I grew in my relationship with Jesus Christ through prayer and Bible study. I learned from the example of mature Christian friends who modeled good habits that rubbed off on me. Instead of making fun of people, I became the first to say something nice about them. People eventually stopped gossiping in front of me, and some stopped gossiping altogether. My new, good habits not only blessed my life, but they rubbed off on others and enriched them too.

Breaking bad habits is hard for a human, but we can ask God to help us. He is our Creator and He cares about us more deeply than we can possibly imagine. He has also provided a role model for us whom we can copy with confidence—His Son, Jesus Christ. Paul points this out to the Philippian believers when he pleads with them to be humble and care about each other's concerns and not just their own. Paul urges them, "Have the same mindset as Christ Jesus: Who, being in very nature God, did not consider equality with God something to be used to his own advantage; rather, he made himself nothing by taking the very nature of a servant, being made in human likeness. And being found in appearance as a man, he humbled himself by becoming obedient to death—even death on a cross!" (Philippians 2:5-8)

Arnold the cat didn't understand how the habits he copied could affect his life. We do, and we can make choices. So why not choose to avoid the copycat blues and copy Jesus instead!

You became imitators of us and of the Lord, for you welcomed the message in the midst of severe suffering with the joy given by the Holy Spirit. And so you became a model to all the believers in Macedonia and Achaia (1 Thessalonians 1:6-7).

Consider This:

Do you have a bad habit you want to work on getting rid of? How did you develop it? How might it be rubbing off on others? Have you thought about what Jesus might do instead? Will you ask God to change you and show you what Scriptures might help?

Jekyll or Hyde?
Heed God's Spirit

There is nothing destroyed by sanctification
but that which would destroy us.

WILLIAM JENKYN

Mooch was a five-year-old kitty orphan when we welcomed him into our home to be a brother to our female cat, Midnight. They adjusted much more slowly than we had anticipated. We attempted to introduce them to the idea of peaceful coexistence, but it was a concept neither of them seemed to comprehend. That meant we had to be present every second they were together, because we couldn't trust them not to fly at each other in a full-fledged fight. Even with our best efforts, we witnessed this far too often for comfort.

After we'd kept them separated for two months, Mooch and Midnight seemed to be adjusting better. They could look at one another through the glass doors without hissing or trying to lunge at each other. We hoped they were getting used to each other's scent by now. So, one particularly warm day, we decided to try them outside together for the first time.

I opened the door and Mooch burst forth ahead of me onto the deck. Midnight was already sunning herself beneath a plastic chair. Her ears perked up and she lifted her head, eyeing Mooch intently. He moved off the deck, and I sat down near Midnight. She seemed to be handling this quite well. As I picked up a book to begin reading, I thought to myself, "Whew! This was a good move after all. It seems to be working." I hadn't gotten past the first page when Mooch decided to return to the deck— and I realized I might have celebrated too soon.

As Mooch ascended the stairs to join us, Midnight snapped to attention. When his paw touched the deck, Midnight the Serene transformed into Midnight the Monster! It was as if she'd been pumped full of air, like an overfilled balloon about to burst. She seemed to swell to twice her normal size and all the hair on her tail stood on end. She was enormous. Even her little face looked huge, and it was dripping with menace. Screeching, she leaped at poor Mooch. He, in turn, froze with one paw still on the deck. This was turning into a Halloween reality show: sweet Midnight blows up into a ball of terror from you know where!

My heart froze too, even as a warning shout burst from my lips: "Stop! Wait!" I feared I was about to witness yet another rolling catfight and their adjustment would be back to square one…separation!

Thankfully, Midnight heeded my cry. Instead of pouncing on Mooch, she ran under another chair on the deck. Mooch, who was still frozen at this point, began to turn as if in slow motion and retreat into the yard.

I was both relieved and delighted that Midnight had heeded my cry. Settling back into my chair, I began to ponder how the Holy Spirit must feel when He whispers to our souls, "Stop! Wait!" as we are about to plunge into sin.

In my own life I've found that instant obedience is the key. If I begin to argue with God in my mind, I'm not obeying, I'm excusing! As a new believer, there was a time when I fought with my husband over chores. I felt put upon and I told him so…over and over again. He didn't agree since he felt he had too much to do from the moment he came through the door until the kids were all asleep. Looking back, I realize we both had too much to do. Raising three kids is no life of ease! The Holy Spirit whispered, "Stop! Wait!" to my soul, but I rationalized that I had to make my point, so I escalated the fight, ignoring that internal warning. Looking back later, I was sad to realize I'd made things worse by grieving the Holy Spirit who was trying to guide me. I was more concerned with my "rights" than with having the right relationship with my husband or with pleasing the Lord. In this way I resembled Midnight the Monster.

Jesus gave up His rights so that He could come to earth as a human and save us. As a follower of Jesus I am to walk in His ways, heeding the Holy Spirit who lives within so He can make me more like Christ. That means giving up my "rights" and trusting Him to guide me in the way of holiness, rather than turning from Jekyll to Hyde by responding according to my old patterns.

Midnight and Mooch share the yard well since they have become brother and sister. They learned to get along because they listened to me and responded in obedience. I'm much better at heeding the Spirit's voice than when I was first a believer. Surrendering to our Master's voice, just as Midnight surrendered to mine, is a learning process that takes time and awareness. But it will save us from grief and bring peace, just as it did for my kitties.

Get rid of all bitterness, rage and anger, brawling and slander, along with every form of malice. Be kind and compassionate to one another, forgiving each other, just as in Christ God forgave you (Ephesians 4:31-32).

Consider This:

Have you heard that small, inner voice of God's Spirit telling you to stop? Did you heed it? What was the result? What helps you listen for His leading? What gets in the way?

When Three Legs
Are Better than Four
Press On and Trust God

*When you come to the end of your
rope, tie a knot and hang on.*

FRANKLIN D. ROOSEVELT

Wolfie and Jen were as close as a cat and a human could be. But they weren't joined at the hip, as the saying goes. They were joined at the leg. Both faced the daunting challenge of a sizable benign leg tumor and refused to be thrown off balance by the obstacles it posed.

Wolfie was a beautiful tiger-striped cat who loved lemon muffins and corn on the cob. He'd go to the trash and fish out muffin wrappers. He'd gobble corn right off the cob as Jen turned it for him. And he loved to express his affection by kneading in her lap or beside her on the floor.

At age ten, Wolfie was diagnosed with a calcium-type tumor on the bone of his right front leg. He had surgery to try to remove it, but it was intertwined with too many parts of his leg for them to get it all. His leg must have kept on hurting, because he wouldn't put weight on it. He couldn't get the full use of it back. He ran around on three legs and his bad leg just seemed in his way. So Jen took him in for a second surgery to remove the leg altogether.

Jen was distraught about the amputation. Not Wolfie. He took his new three-legged status in stride. Jen says his left front leg seemed to center itself and become super-strong. Wolfie got along so well on three legs that people would come to the house and not even notice his missing leg at first.

One day some sort of critter invaded an enclosed outdoor patio area where Wolfie was allowed to go and sun. Wolfie gave chase. The critter scrambled over the high patio wall. Wolfie took a flying leap to follow. He didn't make it—but Jen doubts he would have even with a fourth leg to help him.

Wolfie's courage and resilience were an inspiration to Jen when she faced a severe leg challenge of her own. She was diagnosed with a benign giant cell tumor on her right knee. She had arthroscopic surgery to remove the growth. Afterwards, her surgeon told her that if he'd realized the size of the tumor, he would have chosen a different surgical procedure.

It took Jen a long time to recover, and she had to work through some violent pain in the process. The doctors wanted her to walk right after surgery. She had many hours of physical therapy. The therapists pounded on the knee so it wouldn't develop scar tissue. Unlike her cat she had to drive at a certain point, and at first that hurt, too. It took a year and a half for the leg to feel normal. She was told that she would always have to keep her muscles and quads in shape to keep her leg healthy.

Jen says all this made her feel a special kinship with Wolfie. Like her cat, she refused to give up. She not only resumed her old lifestyle—she started doing even more, participating in swing and salsa dancing.

Wolfie was a plucky, courageous cat—but Jen's love and support surely played a key role in his recovery. Jen's faith in her heavenly Master kept her going as well. That faith was tested a year and a half after Wolfie's leg amputation when Jen finally did lose her beloved kitty—to lung cancer.

Wolfie's death caused Jen violent pain of a different kind. She dropped 11 and a half pounds afterwards. It so happened that was exactly Wolfie's weight when she had him put down. She didn't plan that…it just happened.

Jen recalls that she got very angry with God about Wolfie. She screamed and railed at her Lord. But she held onto God too—and she remembers a point when she actually felt God crying for her and Wolfie. Looking back on that experience, she believes it expanded who God is for her—her view of His love and forbearance. She is awed by the depth of His love—that He cared so much, He absorbed her anger even while He stayed close beside her in her pain.

As I write this, it's Good Friday. Last night I watched a movie with friends about how my Messiah suffered for me. It graphically portrayed the violent pain that Yeshua (Jesus) endured. He was scourged and crucified. Nails were driven into His feet and hands. But He pressed on and refused to give up, taking the punishment for my sins so I could press on to eternal life in Him.

As much as Wolfie and Jen endured, Jesus endured infinitely more. And because He pressed on through His trial, I can take heart and persevere, knowing He has overcome the world.

Dear friends, do not be surprised at the fiery ordeal that has come on you to test you, as though something strange were happening to you. But rejoice inasmuch as you participate in the sufferings of Christ, so that you may be overjoyed when his glory is revealed (1 Peter 4:12-13).

Consider This:

What is the greatest trial you ever faced? What or who helped you? What or who inspired you? How might you encourage and support someone else who is going through a tough time?

Part III

Basking in God's Comfort

MOOCH

Mooch's Loneliest Number
Have Faith in God's Presence

Language...has created the word "loneliness"
to express the pain of being alone. And
it has created the word "solitude" to
express the glory of being alone.

PAUL TILLICH

If a cat could sing pop song lyrics, Mooch would constantly be crooning the tune, "One Is the Loneliest Number." Unlike most cats I've known, he hates to be alone. When my husband Phil goes out to work in the backyard Mooch, who is usually out there sleeping, meows his way over to be with his human. He shadows Phil so closely it's a miracle he hasn't gotten trampled. While Phil is in his greenhouse, Mooch curls up contentedly nearby. If Phil moves to another location, Mooch follows him there too.

It's the same when I come out to water my flowers. Mooch's "talking" begins as soon as he realizes he's not alone. And if I happen to bring a book out to spend time reading, my lap is never empty.

Mooch even runs to our grandchildren, forgetting that they are often his tormentors. I think he just wants to be with someone—even the little ones. Yesterday Eli, who is almost two, made a beeline for

125

Mooch when he spied "his kitty." Longing for any and all attention, Mooch began rubbing against the child's legs, which enabled Eli to grab a handful of fur until I intervened.

Mooch also seeks out the company of our other cat, Midnight. When it's warm outside and she's sunning herself, he settles near her. Since she's a loner and doesn't share his community feelings, Mooch comes as close as he can without causing a growl. Then if she moves, he moves. Mooch simply needs someone nearby.

I think I understand how Mooch feels because I'm his human equivalent. I, too, could croon, "One Is the Loneliest Number." Not everyone would love our community life (five adults, two kids, and two cats under one roof), but for me it's a little taste of heaven.

This was brought home to me recently by an unexpected medical emergency in a strange city. Phil and I had flown across the country to attend a memorial service for his brother's wife. We were visiting with the family when my husband developed an internal "plumbing" problem. Suddenly I found myself in an ambulance with Phil, heading to a hospital that was 3,000 miles from our California home. The EMT was kind and reassuring, but when we reached the emergency room and he left me to sit with Phil, I felt a wave of loneliness sweep over me! True, there were other people around me. But I was lonely for familiar faces—friends to sit with me and a hospital and doctors I knew. Phil was in pain and I felt scared and alone. It was like a bad dream.

When the doctor came to examine Phil, I went out to the hallway to call my daughter so she could alert our friends to pray. When I hung up, loneliness overwhelmed me once more. Tears fell. I left Phil with a nurse and found a bathroom. Ducking inside, I wept as I sought the Lord. "Jesus," I prayed, "I feel completely alone, but I know that's not true because You have promised You will never leave me. I know You are here with me, even if I can't feel Your presence. Please help us both and show us Your great mercy."

And that's just what God did. The doctor fixed Phil up. Three hours later, we were back with his family again, sitting around and chatting as if nothing had ever happened.

Mooch is a cat, and what soothes his loneliness is a physical presence he can see. Our loneliness can be soothed by the presence of God.

Even though this is just as real, we can't always feel Him with us. But we can "reckon" it to be true.

Reckon is one of my favorite words. It means to rely on as real. I usually don't *feel* the presence of the Lord, but I reckon—that is, I rely on the truth—that He is with me because that's what His Word promises. It is true regardless of my feelings. I can't meow my way over to Jesus the way Mooch meows his way over to Phil, but I can reckon on His presence spiritually. Over the years I've found this to be a great use of my imagination as well as a helpful discipline of faith. And that day in the hospital, it was a huge source of comfort. Just as Mooch moved closer to Midnight and us in the physical realm, I moved closer to God spiritually through prayer.

Many centuries ago, a Hebrew warrior named Gideon also needed reassurance of God's presence. Enemies had been oppressing the Israelites. God had allowed it because His people had turned from Him to worship idols. Finally He chose Gideon to save Israel from these pagans. The angel of the Lord came to Gideon and told him the Lord was with him (Judges 6:12). But Gideon wasn't so sure. He asked for a sign. God granted his request. Gideon built God an altar and went on to be His instrument for Israel's deliverance.

We know Mooch needs our physical presence to reassure him that he's not alone. God knows His children need reassurance too. He gave Gideon a sign, and He has given us His Word. We must trust His promises and learn to reckon it true that even when we feel alone, if we belong to God, He is right there with us!

Be strong and courageous. Do not be afraid or terrified because of them, for the LORD your God goes with you; he will never leave you nor forsake you (Deuteronomy 31:6).

Consider This:

If one is your loneliest number, how do you ease your loneliness? Have you ever cried out to Jesus to come near? If you are God's child, can you reckon it true that He will always be with you?

How Cats Drop Anchor
God Steadies Us

To Know the Strength of the Anchor...
You Need to Feel the Storm

Sign on Church Marquee

Mooch and Midnight had just come in from the cold. It was dinnertime and they were wondering where they would find their food this time. As they scurried inside, rubbing my legs so I would know they were hungry, I got their dishes and walked toward the stairs. Climbing the steps, I said, "Tonight I'm feeding you on the landing."

For years our cats led a tranquil life in a household of adults. Then things changed dramatically...toddlers arrived! It was as if a storm hit. Jayden is two, and understands that he's not to touch the kitties, but his idea of getting close to watch them is not the same as their need to be undisturbed. He talks into their faces as if they understand every word. He doesn't get much satisfaction, though, because soon after he appears in the morning they vanish. Eli is 14 months old, and he has no idea what simply watching the kitties means. He adores them, meows at them, and when he gets the chance, grabs hunks of their fur to pet them. The kids are just trying to show their love, but they have inadvertently thrown our cats' world into turmoil.

The result of all this unwanted toddler attention is that Midnight scampers upstairs so she can be protected by the all-important gate at the bottom of the stairway. For Mooch, it's a fast sprint to the cat door and the safety of the great outdoors. That's where they stay until they get hungry.

We have been housing our daughter and her husband for over a year now as he finishes up his schooling. As I watched both cats eating contentedly on the stair landing, I thought about how confusing and out of control their lives have become, and yet how well they've adjusted. They eat contentedly, whether it's on the stair landing as the children stay behind the gate, by the side door if the kids are sitting at the table, or outside if the weather permits. The reason they are doing so well in spite of all the confusion and noise is that they have anchored their security in my husband and me instead of in their circumstances. They find one of us as their tummies begin to growl for food, and they seek out both my husband's and my laps for comfort after the children are tucked into bed. Sometimes they even come into our room to sleep with us. In spite of the storm of toddlers, their anchor in us makes them secure.

We've been in our own "perfect storm" since the economy went south. Our IRA plummeted and the value of our income properties sank. We are housing our daughter's family so we aren't able to make extra income taking in foreign students, as we had before. It seems as though our financial "boat" is about to go under.

As I struggle with my faith in the midst of it all, I've been wishing I were more like my kitties. They simply trust that I will feed them and be there for them. Of course, they are just cats and not aware of all the possible dangers of life; but nevertheless, they trust me more easily than I do my Heavenly Provider, yet He is infinitely more faithful. He has been providing for our needs through believers who were already in our lives, proving Philippians 4:19: "And my God will meet all your needs according to the riches of his glory in Christ Jesus."

Yet because we are still not out of the crisis, I often worry and fret to the point where I get physical and emotional symptoms, and even lose hope. That's when I run to Jesus as my anchor. After prayer, Scripture reading, and confessing my lack of faith, I regain my hope again.

Even so, I wish I were more like my kitties and had their simple trust that doesn't need a boost!

There was a man in Bible times who had a trust problem as well. His son had been the victim of an evil spirit since he was a child. The boy couldn't speak and had seizures. The evil spirit had thrown him into water and fire. This father feared for his son's life. The man sought out Jesus' disciples, but they couldn't rid the boy of his tormentor. Next, the man went to Jesus for aid, pleading, "If you can do anything, take pity on us and help us" (Mark 9:22). Jesus' response was riveting: "'If you can'?…Everything is possible for one who believes" (Mark 9:23).

The father's response is instructive: "I do believe; help me overcome my unbelief!" (Mark 9:24). Part of living in faith is overcoming unbelief, wherever we find it in our life. It can be financial, relational, or emotional. It can be triggered by anything that takes us into a storm, where disappointments of this life rock our faith with devastating waves. But when doubts come, we can drop our anchor in Jesus, because of who He is, what He's done, and what He's promised to do! We can anchor ourselves in the One whose Word assures us that He works in all things for our good and we cannot ever be separated from His love if we belong to Him.

Midnight and Mooch know that when life's storms hit, they can come to us for safety. How much more reliable is our Master! So when life tosses and turns your world, grab onto the Anchor that will never fail to hold you fast!

Because God wanted to make the unchanging nature of his purpose very clear to the heirs of what was promised, he confirmed it with an oath…We have this hope as an anchor for the soul, firm and secure. It enters the inner sanctuary behind the curtain, where Jesus, who went before us, has entered on our behalf (Hebrews 6:17, 19-20).

Consider This:

In what areas of your life do you need to drop anchor in Jesus? What Scriptures might comfort you and help your unbelief? Do you know others being tossed by life's storms whose faith you could encourage?

The Eyes Have It

Look to the Lord

*There is a road from the eye to the heart
that does not go through the intellect.*

G. K. CHESTERTON

There was a time in my childhood when I would walk around the neighborhood looking for Angel. Angel was a sweet stray cat that belonged to everyone and no one. I would often find her in a yard a few houses from my own. This home belonged to a peaceful retired lady. She would sit in her cane-back chair while Angel perched on a four-foot concrete fence that surrounded the woman's backyard. The nice lady would invite me to come and join her. I would sit on the high stool next to the fence and get face to face with Angel and look into her beautiful, great green eyes. We would remain there, face to face, not moving an inch. The calm I felt from looking into Angel's eyes was just phenomenal.

I started doing this at about age ten. In junior high when I felt attacked by my friends, I would find Angel and look into her eyes and cry as I shared my woes. She would quietly listen and let me pet her for a while. In high school I shared with Angel all about the different boys I liked. When I met my future husband, Steve, I told her I knew he was the one for me.

Angel always responded the same way. She would sit quietly and look into my eyes as though she took every word to heart. I will never forget the deep peace that special connection brought me.

My dad's eyes also brought me peace. He was a hardworking man who harvested grain for the farmers in our area. He had three trucks that he used to haul grain, raisin boxes, and other agricultural products.

In 1969, my dad had his first heart attack. I was 17 years old and the only child still living at home. Mom wanted me to call an ambulance, but at first, Dad said no. Finally he gave in. When the emergency team came to our home they put Dad in his recliner and placed the oxygen mask on his face. They asked if I wanted to hold it for him while they had Mom fill out the necessary paperwork. As I sat there with Dad, I knew we were both frightened. But we kept our eyes on one another as I prayed. I'll never forget the smile on his face and the peace in his beautiful blue eyes. He didn't know if he'd live through the night, but he knew that God was in charge. Although no words were spoken, a sweet peace filled the air. Dad was my Angel eyes. And thankfully, he survived.

There is also a marvelous peace that comes from keeping our eyes on the Lord, as Dad and I tried to do that night. David writes in Psalm 25:15, "My eyes are ever on the LORD, for only he will release my feet from the snare." And Hebrews 12:2-3 urges us to "[fix] our eyes on Jesus, the pioneer and perfecter of faith. For the joy set before him he endured the cross, scorning its shame, and sat down at the right hand of the throne of God. Consider him who endured such opposition from sinners, so that you will not grow weary and lose heart."

The apostle Peter had to learn to do this. He once walked on the water toward Jesus. He was fine until he took his eyes off the Messiah. Matthew writes, "But when he saw the wind, he was afraid and, beginning to sink, cried out, 'Lord, save me!' Immediately Jesus reached out his hand and caught him. 'You of little faith,' he said, 'why did you doubt?'" (Matthew 14:30-31)

I love the song "Turn Your Eyes upon Jesus." I can't gaze into His eyes in the same way I could Angel's or my dad's. But I can do this in my mind's eye, through prayer and the Word. I can imagine His eyes filled with love and compassion gazing back at me. And I can receive the marvelous promise in Isaiah 26:3 (NLT), "You will keep in perfect peace all who trust in you, all whose thoughts are fixed on you!"

I lift up my eyes to you, to you who sit enthroned in heaven. As the eyes of slaves look to the hand of their master, as the eyes of a female slave look to the hand of her mistress, so our eyes look to the LORD our God, till he shows us his mercy (Psalm 123:1-2).

Consider This:

In what areas of your life are you fixing your eyes on Jesus? How has this given you peace? In what areas has your gaze wandered? What effect has this had? How might you encourage others to keep their eyes on the Lord?

Liam on Hold

God Is with Us in Limbo

Between the wish and the thing life lies waiting.

Proverb

Liam was in appalling distress. He ran from litter box to sofa and back to litter box, to no avail. He tried desperately to urinate, but couldn't. When he failed to get relief, he ran in circles again. Liam's owners, Tim and Lilly, were frantic with fear. They called their vet, who said to bring him in immediately. They caught him, lovingly put him in his carrier, and rushed him to the cat hospital.

Liam's vet helped relieve his immediate crisis and then talked options to his owners. There were several procedures they could try. But if none of them solved the situation, surgery would be needed. That was hard for Tim and Lilly to hear. Their finances made surgery the very last resort.

Sadly, the vet's first option didn't work so well. One by one, they tried the others. It was a hard time for Tim and Lilly. They had suffered a severe loss in their family. They'd also had to say good-bye to another much older beloved kitty. They didn't want to lose Liam as well. But they were hard-pressed to afford an operation. Still, when all else failed, they opted for surgery anyway because they couldn't bear to let their cherished young orange companion slip away.

Happily, Liam's surgery was successful. But he needed special care and watching afterwards. He had to spend a few days at the cat hospital before going home. Liam, however, didn't understand this. He didn't know why he was being kept in a cage. He didn't know why he was separated from his masters. He was stuck in the cat hospital in "kitty limbo," and it got to him. He stopped eating and seemed depressed. The vet called Tim and Lilly and asked them to come for a visit. As soon as Liam heard them, he let out a howl. Of course, they didn't know for sure what Liam was saying, but they sensed it was, "Get me out of this cage! Rescue me! Now!" Liam was having a rough time of it, and he let his masters know. They realized it wasn't in his best interests to spring him right then, but their presence perked him up. He was able to go home shortly afterwards, and he's been healthy and happy ever since.

My husband Phil and I can identify with Liam. We've been howling to our Master too! We've been in financial limbo, crying out to God, "Get us out of this cage! We need rescue!" Since the recession that began in the fall of 2008, we've seen our life savings plummet. Our IRA dropped by half. Our investment properties sank in value along with the housing market. We were in a financial crisis as urgent as Liam's physical one when Tim and Lilly took him to the hospital. God provided temporary relief through the help of some good friends. But that aid is ending and we are still sick. We need to choose a more lasting procedure to solve our situation and get us back to financial health.

As we explore various options and pray for guidance, we feel like Liam must have in his cage. Unlike Liam, our Master is always with us and we know that. But at times it's hard to feel His presence. And we, like Liam, have gotten depressed in our time of waiting. We want to scream "Enough!" and be freed. Just as Liam needed Tim and Lilly to come to his rescue, we need Jesus to come to ours. We don't like being in our cage of limbo even though we understand that God's timing is perfect.

Many centuries ago, a woman named Hannah was also in limbo (1 Samuel 1). She was in the barren woman "cage," desperate to get pregnant. Being childless was a stigma at that time because it was thought to be a sign of God's disfavor.

Hannah was married to a man named Elkanah. Polygamy was common then, and he had another wife too. He loved Hannah more, but that didn't compensate for her deep desire to carry and give birth to a child. She was distressed, but she didn't give up. She went to the temple year after year, fell on her face, and cried out to God. She knew it was in God's power to get her out of her "cage" and believed He would hear her prayers. Finally God granted her request, and she gave birth to Samuel, who became one of the Lord's great prophets. God then blessed Hannah with more children as well.

As Phil and I go through the Scriptures and keep praying about our financial distress, we feel the struggle of holding onto our faith. Even as we cry out for rescue, like Liam, we long to emulate Hannah. Anxious as we are to get out of this cage of uncertainty, there is something very beautiful in this awful waiting time. We sense that we are developing a deeper nearness to the One who holds our future. Just as Liam perked up when he saw Tim and Lilly, so we perk up as we spend time pouring our hearts out to God. Even though we aren't sure what will happen, we know that He has heard us. We hope the end of our story will be a good one, as was Liam's and Hannah's when they were released from their limbo. In the meantime, through the tears and angst, we are experiencing the presence of our faithful God in the midst of our "cage."

Consider it pure joy, my brothers and sisters, whenever you face trials of many kinds, because you know that the testing of your faith produces perseverance. Let perseverance finish its work so that you may be mature and complete, not lacking anything (James 1:2-4).

Consider This:

Have you ever been in a limbo situation where God kept you waiting? Did you experience God's presence in your "cage"? What was hardest about trusting Him? Did you respond more like Hannah or Liam? How has that affected your walk with God?

Cat "Replacement" Therapy
God Leads Us Through Loss

God didn't promise days without pain,
laughter without sorrow, sun without rain,
but He did promise strength for the day,
comfort for the tears, and light for the way.

AUTHOR UNKNOWN

My friend Hailey still remembers the day Oscar first showed up. The furthest thing from her mind was a new little feline. She and her husband were "owned" by Kitty, who in their safe neighborhood had the privilege of spending time outdoors. When she heard meowing outside, Hailey figured Kitty wanted in. She was engrossed in TV, and was watching even as she opened the door. Not till later did she realize she'd let in a kitten she'd never laid eyes on before.

Since the little fellow wasn't hers, she put him outdoors again, hoping he'd wander back to wherever he'd come from. There was also Kitty to think about. She had been an only cat for many years, and Hailey doubted she'd want to share her humans' affections with another feline at this point in her life. But the kitten would not give up. He stuck around, mewing for admittance all night. By next morning, he was under the house. Hailey and her husband tried to coax him out. No go.

Then, as her hubby was about to turn on the dishwasher, Hailey saw a paw reaching out from under it.

"Stop!"

They pushed the kitten's paw back through a hole in the floor, lured him out from under their home, and welcomed Oscar into their lives.

As they had feared, Kitty wasn't pleased—or so they thought. She stopped "talking" to them. She wouldn't eat. They tried hand-feeding her, but it wasn't helping. Then they began to suspect that more than Oscar was to blame. They took Kitty to the vet and learned she had cancer. She died the next day. Oscar blessed their lives for many glorious years and became one of their most special kitties ever!

Hailey feels Oscar was a gift from God. She didn't know Kitty's days were numbered, but He did. She sees Oscar as His provision, not to replace Kitty, but to help fill the loss-shaped hole her cat's passing left.

I have felt God's precious care in a similar, yet different way. Not quite ten years ago, I lost my treasured best friend. Maxine's death was sudden and abrupt and none of us saw it coming. She passed away just after Thanksgiving. Christmas was coming. I'd spent Christmas Eve with Maxine and her family for years. But with her passing so fresh, her husband and children wanted to do something different that year and be alone. I understood.

A newer friend reached out to me. Dottie was the Teaching Director of my Community Bible Study class. We'd become closer as I'd served on the class Leaders Council. Dottie invited me to her home for Christmas Eve. It was a totally different but delightful experience. Their delicious potluck meal, performance time, and hilarious acted-out version of "The Twelve Days of Christmas" blessed my heart on that night and on every Christmas Eve since. Even more special, over the years Dottie has become my new best friend, and she's one of my coauthors on this very book.

Dottie will never replace the dear friend whose memory I will forever treasure. But, as with Oscar and Hailey, God had Dottie waiting in my life to fill a sudden loss-shaped hole. And like Oscar, she put arms and legs on God's comfort in a time of pain and grief—and became a rich, ongoing blessing.

Jesus knew that His own death on the cross would devastate those who loved and followed Him. He promised His disciples that He would send the Holy Spirit to comfort and guide them. But there was also one individual who would suffer a very special and unique loss-shaped hole in her life—His mother, Mary. Fortunately, the Lord had made loving provision for that, too. In the Gospel of John we read, "When Jesus saw his mother there, and the disciple whom he loved standing nearby, he said to her, 'Woman, here is your son,' and to the disciple, 'Here is your mother.' From that time on, this disciple took her into his home" (John 19:26-27).

The Bible tells us that death came into the world through sin. Loss wasn't part of God's original plan. And one day when Jesus returns and God makes us and all creation new, such things will pass away—but not yet.

In the meantime, God's provision of Oscar and Dottie speaks volumes to me about His love and care. He knows the losses we will face and just what we need to sustain us. He is the God of all comfort, and will hold us close and lead us through if we put our faith in Him.

Praise be to the God and Father of our Lord Jesus Christ, the Father of compassion and the God of all comfort, who comforts us in all our troubles, so that we can comfort those in any trouble with the comfort we ourselves receive from God. For just as we share abundantly in the sufferings of Christ, so also our comfort abounds through Christ (2 Corinthians 1:3-5).

Consider This:

Have you experienced God's care and comfort during a time of loss? What did He do? How did it help you through? Is there a loss you're struggling with? Would you pray, pour out your hurt, and open your heart to His healing touch?

Midnight's Vanishing Act
God Restores

*By a Carpenter mankind was made,
and only by that Carpenter can
mankind be remade.*

DESIDERIUS ERASMUS

Midnight loves to go out and sun. On this beautiful morning, we were only too happy to let her. It was 10 AM and we figured she'd want in by noon. We were a bit perturbed when noon came and went with no sign of our cat. Our concern grew as the clock kept ticking. By 4 PM we were scared. This was not like Midnight at all. Normally she goes in and out all day. We recalled how she'd been lethargic the previous day and wondered if there was more to it than we'd thought. What if something awful was wrong and she'd crawled off somewhere to die?

I had to leave for an evening Bible study class that I teach, so I asked my son, Matthew, to keep watch. He lives nearby and loves this kitty as much, if not more, than I do. I called Matthew the instant class ended. Midnight was still missing. We both began to grieve, fearing she was gone for good. I asked God to help her if she was alive, and to help us if she wasn't. As I was closing up after Bible study, I tried to steel myself for returning to a house that would be missing my little black kitty.

But instead I heard my phone ring with a wonderful surprise. Matthew's voice was filled with joy as he said, "She's here! She's back!"

Matthew had been heading to the living room to join his sister Sarah. He glanced at the staircase and spied our missing cat. Midnight was sitting right there on the steps. Matthew was so overwhelmed that he stuttered as he cried out the news. Sarah got up to make sure he wasn't hallucinating. But it was true. Midnight looked completely normal, as if she'd been planted on those steps all day. She had apparently slipped in at some earlier point and was now waiting to be fed, completely oblivious to what she had put us through. We felt as though we'd received her back from the dead!

Midnight wasn't the first family member I'd felt that way about. God had miraculously restored my husband too. A few months prior to this, Phil had undergone heart bypass surgery, and it had been far from routine. Phil's heart stopped not once, but twice. It flatlined, meaning there was no pulsing whatsoever. His doctors managed to get his heart beating again and perform the surgery. But they gave us ominous news. Since they had no idea how much time had elapsed when his heart wasn't pumping blood, there was a chance Phil had suffered brain damage. He might even be brain dead.

One of Phil's surgeons said it could take up to 72 hours before he awoke and they could tell more of what was going on. He also urged me not to give up hope. He'd seen people declared brain dead who'd "come back" in a week. Still, it was very hard news to receive. The whole family left the hospital in grief that day. My son-in-law, Dan, took my hand as I wept. He held it all the way to the car. I told the Lord, "I just don't think I can wait that long!"

Thankfully, I didn't have to. We had been home just a brief time when the ICU nurse called to say Phil was awake. He had moved every body part she asked him to, and successfully answered her questions by nodding his head. There was no brain damage.

Just as Midnight suddenly showed up on our stairs, relieving our fears, so Phil woke up relieving our fears just 45 minutes after we had left him at the hospital. In both cases the disasters we dreaded did not happen, and by God's grace our loved ones were restored to us.

There is a wonderful story of restoration in the Gospel of Luke. A widow in the town of Nain lost her only child, a son. Her grief over her son's death was bad enough, but at that time it also meant she was doomed to poverty, since widows couldn't own anything. Jesus, His disciples, and a large crowd that was following him approached the town gate right when this man's body was being carried out for burial. Scripture tells us that when Jesus saw the scene, "his heart went out to her and he said, 'Don't cry.' Then he went up and touched the bier they were carrying him on, and the bearers stood still. He said, 'Young man, I say to you, get up!' The dead man sat up and began to talk, and Jesus gave him back to his mother" (Luke 7:13-15).

I think God sometimes restores in such ways to give us a glimpse of what will happen when Jesus returns to restore and make all things new. God's original creation was perfect. But then Adam and Eve disobeyed God and sin entered the world. Mankind and the rest of creation was tainted. But one day Jesus, also called the last Adam, will restore God's perfection again. That is when we shall "bear the image of the heavenly man" (1 Corinthians 15:49) and the last enemy, death, will be destroyed (1 Corinthians 15:26).

I'm delighted that Midnight and Phil were restored to me, but these were just foretastes of God's infinitely greater restoration to come. We as believers long for this and look forward to enjoying it with our precious Lord Jesus forever!

I saw the Holy City, the new Jerusalem, coming down out of heaven from God, prepared as a bride beautifully dressed for her husband. And I heard a loud voice from the throne saying, "Look! God's dwelling place is now among the people, and he will dwell with them. They will be his people, and God himself will be with them and be their God. He will wipe every tear from their eyes. There will be no more death or mourning or crying or pain, for the old order of things has passed away." He who was seated on the throne said, "I am making everything new!" (Revelation 21:2-5).

Consider This:

Have you ever had something you gave up for lost restored to you? What happened? How did it affect the way you see God? What are you most looking forward to about how God will restore His children and all creation for eternity?

Full House

God Made Us for Each Other

The most terrible poverty is loneliness,
and the feeling of being unloved.

MOTHER TERESA

Midnight is my all-time favorite cat. She got separated from her feline mom at around four weeks of age and somehow ended up on our backyard hill. After she got over being afraid of us, she "owned" us as her people. We think being lost and all alone at such a young age made her happier than most cats to have a family. That was 14 years ago and she still loves being part of our household...especially when we're eating chicken!

Our typical family dinner includes five adults, two children, often a guest, and one begging cat. You guessed it: Midnight. It can be very lively, especially when Midnight mixes in. When she likes what we are serving, chicken being her favorite, she sits on the floor near one of her people and eats as much as we give her. If that doesn't satisfy her, she stretches out with her hind legs on the floor and her paws on the edge of the table to urge us to share more. It is a funny sight to see the head of a little cat rise at the edge of the table with both of her front paws framing her face. She even bats the closest hand with her paw to make sure we know she's there. When the children see her antics, they giggle with delight. Midnight is as different from the frightened kitten we found alone on the hill many years ago as day is from night. She's a secure and vital part of our family.

On one particular evening, Midnight had successfully begged some chicken from us. It was Wednesday. Stephanie, one member of our household, gets home late for dinner that day, so we always leave out her portion to reheat. She hates this evening because she doesn't like eating alone and she misses the excitement and noise of the family meal. It makes her feel lonely.

Stephanie set her plate on the table and went to the kitchen for a glass of water. She returned to find a shocking sight. Midnight was sitting politely across from her food, right on the opposite placemat. Aside from the cat and Stephanie's meal, the table that normally seats eight was completely empty. Stephanie called us to come see her new dinner companion. We all chuckled and joked that Midnight, having known what it was to be lonely, didn't want Stephanie to have to eat all by herself.

Loneliness was a pressing problem for Stephanie when we first met her. She was living in an apartment and pursuing her Master's degree. She was not only alone, but lonely—and that's exactly what she told God. She didn't really pray, or even expect for one moment that she would be given a solution. She was merely sharing her deep feelings with the Lord.

Loneliness is a difficult thing. God made us social creatures and we need companionship. When Adam was created, God said it wasn't good for him to be alone, even though he "walked" with God each evening. We all need alone time, a time for solitude; but the empty, haunting feeling of loneliness isn't the same, and it's not good.

During the next year, as my husband Phil and I got to know Stephanie better, we invited her to live with us. We could use the extra income, and she could use the extra people to keep her from loneliness. A few months after she moved in, our daughter, her husband, and their little baby joined us as our son-in-law pursued his education. It wasn't long before our daughter's surprise pregnancy added yet another person to our home. Now the five-bedroom house that a year ago had been too big for us was bursting at the seams. We have needed to make adjustments as we've learned what each other's needs are, but we have done amazingly well in becoming a family. And best of all, loneliness is something we simply don't experience right now. We are happy to be a community. We tell others that God made us a family...and that includes our kitties!

God made Ruth part of Naomi's family too, a long, long time ago. Naomi and her husband and sons had left their home in Bethlehem to settle in Moab because Israel was experiencing a famine. Their two sons married Moabite women. But in just ten years all three men had died. Naomi was left in Moab with her two daughters-in-law. So when she heard that Israel's famine had ended, she decided to return to her homeland. She was very kind and released both of her daughters-in-law, saying, "Go back, each of you, to your mother's home. May the LORD show you kindness, as you have shown kindness to your dead husbands and to me. May the LORD grant that each of you will find rest in the home of another husband" (Ruth 1:8-9). They all wept as Orpah gave her mother-in-law a farewell kiss. But Ruth hung onto Naomi and spoke the now famous words, "Where you go I will go, and where you stay I will stay. Your people will be my people and your God my God" (Ruth 1:16).

It's not hard to imagine that Naomi was overwhelmed with gratitude that she wouldn't have to travel the treacherous roads by herself. But more than that, Naomi was spared from being completely alone and lonely. Just as Midnight's loneliness ended when we caught her on our hill, and just as Stephanie's loneliness ended when she moved in, so Naomi's loneliness was abated when Ruth refused to leave her.

That night when Midnight sat on the table waiting for Stephanie, we all wondered if she simply wanted more food, or if she was motivated by a desire to keep her human friend company. Stephanie prefers the latter notion because she believes that Midnight may have been marked by the frightening experience of being all alone as a kitten. Midnight is a cat, so she couldn't share her feelings with her Maker the way Stephanie did. But God knew, and provided her with a family—us! If we are lonely and we talk to Him about it, He will give us exactly what we need. It may be a friend, or pets, or even getting to know Him better. God loves us and He knows our needs even before we ask. Midnight and Stephanie are living proof!

God sets the lonely in families (Psalm 68:6).

Consider This:

Have you ever experienced deep loneliness in your life? What caused it? How was it resolved? If you're lonely now, have you talked with God about it? Do you know someone else who is lonely that you could reach out to?

A Time to Die
God Holds Us in His Hands

*Life and death are balanced
on the edge of a razor.*

HOMER

In Ecclesiastes, it says everything under heaven has its appointed time, including death. Barney put a kitty exclamation point on that truth. As cats go he was a very senior citizen. He lasted over 19 years and battled kidney failure at the end...but one day he was finally done.

On that last day, Barney turned a corner. I rushed him to the vet and she confirmed it was time to put him down. I decided to take him home and spend a few hours saying good-bye before sending him to his final reward.

God and Barney had other plans.

I wasn't home 20 minutes before I knew I mustn't wait. He could barely move and was moaning. I took him back to the vet and said, "Do it now!" As I held him and he relaxed, no longer in pain and at peace at last, I knew I had done right by him.

A dear friend and Bible teacher has often pointed out that suffering is not redemptive in animals. There is no gain in prolonging their pain.

151

God has given mankind stewardship over them, and as Barney's guardian, I was responsible for making the merciful choice.

Human beings are a very different story. Scripture tells us only God has the right to terminate a person's life. But today we have the means to artificially prolong human life...perhaps beyond what God might intend. Sometimes the kindest thing is to stop extreme measures and let the person go—and that's what happened with my mother.

Like Barney, Mom had already lived to a very ripe old age. She was 91, and had battled chronic leukemia for years. A few months earlier, she had suffered a severe heart attack. She had miraculously lived through surgery to fix some blockages and I hoped we'd bought her at least a couple of years.

God knew five and a half months was more like it.

Mom was a fighter. She wanted to live. But her body was done, just like Barney's. In a period of less than two weeks, she had multiple episodes of congestive heart failure. She would be rushed to the hospital, they'd save her and get her stable, she'd go home, and hours later she'd be back in an ambulance. Then the crises started happening in the hospital before she could even get home. Her own determination wavered and she told me she was tired and didn't really care which way things went.

Finally, her cardiologist had a talk with me. He told me he thought it was time to put her on hospice. Her heart was tired, and it simply couldn't hang on any longer. We spoke with Mom and she agreed.

I hadn't known a whole lot about hospice, but I am eternally grateful for the comfort it provided Mom. Her greatest wish was to be at home, and she was able to go there and stay there. Medication and equipment was provided to keep her comfortable and, should she go into congestive heart failure again, ease her pain and suffering. She also retained the dignity of choice. She could change her mind and go off hospice at any point.

Mom returned from the hospital on a Thursday afternoon. She had tea that evening in her beloved dining room. Friday night one of her nurses wheeled her through the garden she loved. Saturday morning she once again went into heart failure, but her nurse had medication at hand to ease her pain and her doctor hurried to her home to be with her also.

I had left Friday to return to my own home for 24 hours. I rushed back to be at her side. She was still responsive and lucid, but soon slipped into a coma. Over the next day or so, she lay peaceful and quiet as her body slowly shut down. Twenty minutes before midnight on Sunday, less than four days after going on hospice care, she passed into the Lord's presence.

Losing loved ones is never easy, but I was comforted that like Barney, Mom's passing was a mercy. She had lived long and finished her race and her time was in God's hands. But best of all, I knew Mom had come to know her Messiah, and one day we would meet again in God's presence.

Scripture says that not only is there a time to be born and a time to die, but there is a time to be born again. In John 3, Jesus explained we must be born not just physically, but spiritually as well. And in John 5:24, Jesus said, "Very truly I tell you, whoever hears my word and believes him who sent me has eternal life and will not be judged but has crossed over from death to life."

Has it been your time to be born again? If so, your time to die will be a doorway to eternal life in Christ.

One of the criminals who hung there hurled insults at him: "Aren't you the Messiah? Save yourself and us!" But the other criminal rebuked him. "Don't you fear God," he said, "since you are under the same sentence? We are punished justly, for we are getting what our deeds deserve. But this man has done nothing wrong." Then he said, "Jesus, remember me when you come into your kingdom." Jesus answered him, "Truly I tell you, today you will be with me in paradise" (Luke 23:39-43).

Consider This:

What about death do you find most frightening? Most saddening? Most comforting? If it were your time to die, do you know you would step into God's presence? If not, do you want to take time to be born again right now by asking Jesus to come into your heart, forgive your sins, and be your Lord and Savior?

The Unexpected Hug
God Lifts Us Up

*You can't wrap love in a box, but you
can wrap a person in a hug.*

AUTHOR UNKNOWN

Brooke's cat Chloe was a Cornish Rex. This breed looks to some like it came from outer space, but it really came from Cornwall, England. These cats have small heads, big ears, and very soft short fur. Though they may not look like cuddlers, they love people and are very affectionate.

God knew just what Brooke needed and that Chloe was the "purrfect" cat for her. She had been married for many years to the man who she thought held her heart. But over time, there had been unexpected journeys and poor decisions along life's road. Now her husband had left her. The children were grown and the house was empty except for Brooke and Chloe.

One day as Brooke walked down a supermarket aisle, a wave of sadness washed over her about her impending divorce. She stopped, bowed her head, and prayed for a hug. Brooke went home, unloaded her groceries, and helped herself to a nice glass of iced tea. She sat on her couch watching Chloe roam the house as she reflected on her own life. She thought about how the Cornish Rex breed was unique and sometimes misunderstood—and compared herself to her cat.

Suddenly Chloe sprang onto Brooke's lap. Wrapping her paws around Brooke's neck while nuzzling against her cheek, she gave Brooke a big, affectionate hug. In nine years, this cat had never done anything like that.

Brooke realized the Lord had just sent her a hug. She looked up and prayed, "God, it wasn't what I imagined, but it surely did work!"

I feel God's hugs too. I need them often, and He obliges. Several weeks ago, I was stressed about my daughter's wedding. I felt anxious about getting everything done. While I was shopping, I started talking to the woman ahead of me in the checkout line. She commented that what I was buying looked like it would make many people happy. By her sweet spirit, I sensed she was a believer in Jesus. I responded with a hearty "Amen!" She laughed and concurred. We talked all the way to our cars, exchanged phone numbers, and planned on meeting again soon. She even prayed for me. She sensed I really needed encouragement, and gave it. Now that was a wonderful unexpected "hug"!

I think Jesus gave unexpected hugs when He walked this earth. One was to the woman taken in adultery. He was teaching in the temple courts when she was brought before Him. The religious leaders asked if she should be stoned, as the law directed. Jesus gave the now famous answer, "Let any one of you who is without sin be the first to throw a stone at her" (John 8:7). Her accusers melted away. Only Jesus and the woman were left. John writes, "Jesus straightened up and asked her, 'Woman, where are they? Has no one condemned you?' 'No one, sir,' she said. 'Then neither do I condemn you,' Jesus declared. 'Go now and leave your life of sin'" (John 8:10-11). Surely that woman felt an unexpected hug, though she may not have called it that!

Brooke asked God for encouragement and He hugged her through her cat. God "hugged" me through a new friend in a grocery store line. And many centuries ago, a woman bereft and in sin received a very special hug from Jesus—the embrace of His grace.

We serve a loving, compassionate God who is eager to uplift and encourage us. He also asks us to do this for others in His name. So ask for His hugs, receive them with joy and thanksgiving, and pass them along.

May our Lord Jesus Christ himself and God our Father, who loved us and by his grace gave us eternal encouragement and good hope, encourage your hearts and strengthen you in every good deed and word (2 Thessalonians 2:16-17).

Consider This:

When was the last time you got an unexpected hug from God or a friend? What happened? How did it encourage you? How might you give someone else an unexpected hug?

Part IV

Lapping up God's Wisdom

MUFFIN

Chasing Shadows
God Is Our Reality Check

How many legs does a dog have if
you call the tail a leg? Four. Calling
a tail a leg doesn't make it a leg.

ABRAHAM LINCOLN

Muffin is a beautiful seal point Ragdoll with a healthy kitty instinct to chase things. Moving objects that elude her grasp are tantalizing. I have purchased cat toys that were essentially long sticks with something fluffy or feathery hanging from their end, and had great fun getting her and other kitties to race after them and bat at this "prey." Eventually I'd drop the stick and they'd grab the prize.

Such a toy was nowhere in sight when Muffin started lunging at something whose identity was a total mystery to me. To my amazement and amusement, what I finally discovered was that my kitty was chasing a shadow. I was wearing a watch, and its face was reflected on certain surfaces around me. As my hand moved, the watch face cast a small, round, moving shadow. Muffin was going after this without the slightest clue that what she was stalking wasn't even real.

It's interesting to contemplate what this activity did and didn't do. It certainly gave Muffin some great exercise. However briefly, it amused and occupied her. But if she had been a homeless street cat, needing to hunt to eat, that shadow couldn't have fed her. And depending on how my hand moved and where that shadow went, it might possibly have lured Muffin into kitty acrobatics that put her at risk. But since Muffin is a well-fed pet and I made sure her shadow toy didn't get her into trouble, her pursuit of unreality was only harmless fun.

Muffin the cat is not alone in chasing after shadows. We humans do it too. And although we are usually far more aware than my kitty, if we're not careful harmless fun can become an escape that holds back our growth.

My friend Mia believes this is exactly what happened to her. She had childhood experiences that damaged her sense of self-worth. A failed marriage and a job that was less than fulfilling didn't help. Mia's real life wasn't awful, but it wasn't what she longed for. So she created a shadow world in her daydreams and retreated into it to escape her pain. She imagined a life for herself that satisfied her deepest unfulfilled longings. She created fictional Italian grandparents who lived in a beautiful villa in northern California. She'd fantasize about going there to visit, hanging out with them in their huge kitchen, and making fabulous food together. She also had a pretend brother who watched out for her and gave her advice. These inventions were attempts to satisfy her longing for love and security.

Mia's shadow world was fun. It distracted her from her grief. But it didn't help her work through her painful emotions. It not only didn't help her grow as a person, it was getting in the way. It also didn't change anything in her actual life—it just gave her a place to go and hide from what she was struggling with and feeling.

Fortunately, Mia loves Jesus and has given her heart to Him. God's Holy Spirit is at work in her. She also has Christian friends who love and care about her and interact with her about her life. And God's Word is constantly confronting her with His perspective on reality, and His truth.

Those influences, and her own unwillingness to succumb to ongoing depression, have spurred her to start dealing with her feelings. Hard as it is, she is working with a therapist. She is acknowledging that lasting answers don't lie in running away to a shadow world, but in learning to deal with the real one.

Even more significant, she is learning that God's reality offers far more hope and encouragement than "pretend fulfillment." Through her study of His Word and the input of caring believers, she is being infused with God's truth. Part of that truth is that He is at work transforming each of His children into His masterpiece—a person of beautiful character with all the needed tools to fulfill God's unique purpose for each of us. Even if Mia is still being dragged down by Satan's lies and accusations, she at least knows they are lies—and is being helped to fight back. She has the prayer support of friends who regularly lift her up. And as she deals with her pain in the real world, she is finding that she is retreating into her pretend world less and less.

King Nebuchadnezzar of Babylon lived in a shadow world of a different kind. He thought his greatness was due to himself and not to God. Despite a warning dream from God interpreted by the prophet Daniel, Nebuchadnezzar persisted in his prideful delusion. In response, God gave this king a huge reality check. He lost his mind and lived as an animal. Finally he bowed his heart and acknowledged God—at which point his sanity and his kingdom were restored (Daniel 4).

Muffin the cat may get confused about the line between shadow and reality. But I know where it is, and I'm her master. I am her reality check. And God is ours! Not just Mia, but all of us, can chase shadows instead of reality, and this can take many forms. I have sought self-worth and fulfillment in a writing career that only a deeper walk with the Lord could bring. Seeking the things of this world over the riches of God and His Kingdom is chasing shadows in a whole different way. And it is just as empty and self-defeating.

I am grateful that God is real! I am grateful that His truth is slowly freeing me from the shadows that hold me back. And I am looking forward to when I will enter His presence, fully transformed, to enjoy the reality of an eternity with Him.

The law is only a shadow of the good things that are coming—not the realities themselves. For this reason it can never, by the same sacrifices repeated endlessly year after year, make perfect those who draw near to worship (Hebrews 10:1).

Consider This:

Are you chasing shadows in your life? What are they? What makes them attractive? How might they be holding you back? Are there any shadows you've let go of? What freed you?

The Cat Fight That Wasn't
Choose Peace

Peace is not merely a distant goal that we seek,
but a means by which we arrive at that goal.

MARTIN LUTHER KING JR.

Mooch was having a howling fight with another cat in our backyard. Our son Matthew was visiting that day, so he went to check things out. When he opened the side door, the other cat fled. Mooch was left standing his ground alone when Midnight, our other kitty, came out to investigate the noise. Maybe she smelled the feline intruder as she looked at Mooch. Whatever the reason, she seemed to view *him* as the aggressive stranger. We're not sure what was going on in her little cat brain, but the screech she let out was enough to alert the whole neighborhood that there was a problem. She made more huge angry noises as her fur stood on end. Mooch stared at Midnight with a look of amazement. Even though Mooch was the "kitty come lately" in our home, he and Midnight had learned to live together—so her behavior probably bewildered him. Before Matthew had a chance to step in, Midnight lowered her head to the ground, let out a horrid, blood-curdling shriek, and charged.

Mooch could have fought her, but instead he leaped backwards,

165

turned around, and walked slowly and deliberately into the bushes at the edge of our yard. He remained there for hours as she sniffed every square inch of grass, looking for the intruder she thought she had to fight. Mooch's actions avoided what could have been an ugly encounter. When he finally did come in, Midnight seemed to know who he was and acted completely normal again. Mooch had avoided a potential battle by simply removing himself and giving it time.

I wish all Christians would live like Mooch! Some do, but I see others acting like Midnight, bristling in anger and wrath. They seem unwilling or unable to heed what the Bible has to say and turn the other cheek.

Fortunately, Sara was one Christian who followed Mooch's example. She fell madly in love with a young man named Ryan. He seemed to feel the same way about her—at least at first. They worked at the same church in youth ministry. This made things all the more wonderful. After a few months together, they talked of marriage and started ring shopping.

It was at this point that Ryan got cold feet. Actually, his feet got more than cold—they got icy! He told Sara the bad news that they were no longer a couple. She was devastated. Her dreams were shattered. And to make matters worse, they still had to work together!

Sara could have fought back, but she didn't. She chose to act biblically, work on forgiveness, and honor the Lord. At first, it was a sheer act of her will. She resisted the temptation to blame Ryan for rejecting her. She refused to call him a "jerk" to her friends. Instead, she protected his reputation by simply saying they had a change of plans. She thought of running away from her job, but hard as it was she chose to stick with the ministry for the sake of the kids involved. That meant she would still be working alongside Ryan several times a week. She experienced hard feelings toward Ryan, but she never gave in to them. What Mooch did on a physical level, Sara did emotionally—she leaped backwards and walked away to give it time. And in due course, she and Ryan became friends again—all because she chose not to fight.

David is a striking biblical example of someone who chose not to fight when his rights were violated. When he was still a shepherd boy, God selected him to be the next king of Israel. The great prophet Samuel anointed him in the presence of his brothers. After that, David entered the service of the current king, Saul. In time, David eclipsed Saul in the people's esteem. Saul guessed David might be God's replacement king, so he lashed out and tried to kill David, forcing David to flee for his life.

David was a fugitive for years. On one occasion, Saul was hunting him with 3,000 men (1 Samuel 24). Saul entered a cave to relieve himself, not knowing David and his forces were already deep inside. David's men urged him to seize his chance and kill Saul, but he refused. Instead, he walked away and gave it time—time for God to judge between him and Saul and bring about a change in kingship in His own sovereign way. And that is just what happened.

We don't know why Mooch backed off from Midnight's attack. Did he understand they were family when he chose not to fight? We're not sure. All we know is that Mooch turned his kitty cheek and things got better. Sara and David also turned away from conflict, and in so doing, honored the Lord.

What about us? Will we screech and charge others to protect our rights or seek vengeance? Or will we please God by forgiving, leaving vengeance to Him, and choosing peace instead?

You have heard that it was said, "Eye for eye, and tooth for tooth." But I tell you, do not resist an evil person. If anyone slaps you on the right cheek, turn to them the other also. And if anyone wants to sue you and take your shirt, hand over your coat as well. If anyone forces you to go one mile, go with them two miles (Matthew 5:38-41).

Consider This:

When was the last time you had to choose between fighting and backing away? What did you feel like doing? What did you actually do? What was the result?

Chickee's Lost Tail
Temptation Bites

Do not bite at the bait of pleasure, till
you know there is no hook beneath it.

THOMAS JEFFERSON

Chickee is a cat that lives in Glenn and Susie Myers' backyard. This one-acre yard is a beehive of activity. It has a workshop, a vegetable garden, and pens for pigs and chickens. Various animals have taken up residence there. During a time when there weren't chickens, a cat took over a vacant pen. She seemed so comfortable there that Glenn and Susie changed her name to Chickee to suit her surroundings.

At the time, the Myers also had a big yellow dog "on loan." A friend was moving and had no place to put him. Glenn and Susie offered to keep him as long as there was a need. They didn't realize that Rad (short for Rent-a-Dog) loved to chase critters—including cats.

Chickee wasn't completely innocent in Rad's wrongdoing. This dog was a huge temptation to her. She loved to taunt him as she wandered around in the yard. Then he'd run after her—and the chase was on. She would race to the chicken pen with Rad on her heels, jump over its fence and dive down a pipe inside. Rad could get over the fence but not down the pipe, so she was safe. He'd abandon the pursuit and leave, she'd rest awhile, then go back to taunting him again. This cycle was repeated many times.

One day, Chickee wasn't at the top of her game. She walked around Rad as usual, daring him to chase her. When he did take after her, she thought she was up for the challenge. Chickee hightailed it across the yard and over the fence into the pipe—but not quite fast enough. Just as her tail was crossing the safety zone, Rad grabbed it in his teeth. The results were not pretty.

Glenn and Susie raced to Chickee's aid. They rushed her to the vet. Chickee survived, but her tail didn't. It had to be amputated.

Playing with temptation is something God's Word tells us not to do. It urges us to flee instead. Chickee let herself be lured by temptation and didn't flee in time. She lost her tail. We have some friends who also toyed with temptation and got bitten by it. Their temptation was to buy a new home they couldn't really afford.

They were young and impatient to start living the American dream. That meant a new home, two cars, and lots of toys. They were in over their heads but thought they could make it if they were careful. But like Chickee, a time came when they couldn't quite get down the pipe to safety. Because of the economy, the husband lost his job. Because of his higher education, it was hard to find a new one. He was over-qualified for most of the jobs that were available. Times got harder. After much prayer and sadness, our friends were forced to downsize. They had to get rid of their expensive toys. They had to make do with one car for a time. They had to sell their home and buy a smaller, more affordable one. They felt like their tails had been bitten off. But they now have work and hope. And now that they have fled temptation, they are happy and content to be living more within their means.

Ananias and Sapphira weren't so lucky. This first-century couple played with temptation too. In Acts 5 we read that they sold some property and claimed they were giving all the proceeds to the early church. But in fact, they were holding some back. Perhaps their temptation was to get big reputations for generosity on false pretenses. But in the process they were taunting not a big yellow dog, but God Himself.

We don't know whether God revealed this to the apostle Peter or he found out some other way—but he learned the truth. He confronted

Ananias, saying, "Ananias, how is it that Satan has so filled your heart that you have lied to the Holy Spirit and have kept for yourself some of the money you received for the land? Didn't it belong to you before it was sold? And after it was sold, wasn't the money at your disposal? What made you think of doing such a thing? You have not lied just to human beings but to God" (Acts 5:3-4). Ananias fell dead when he heard this. Hours later, his wife met the same fate.

Chickee was tempted to taunt a dog and gave in. She lost her tail. Our friends ran to their irresponsible dream. They spent more money than they had, got bitten by their debt, and lost what they owned. Ananias and Sapphira were tempted by pride and lied to God. They suffered the ultimate bite of sin—death!

God doesn't want us to get bitten. He urges us to flee temptation for our good. And if we stumble, He offers a way out. We can come to Him, tell the truth, confess our sin, and receive the forgiveness He freely offers us through faith in Christ—our ultimate safety pipe.

So, if you think you are standing firm, be careful that you don't fall! No temptation has overtaken you except what is common to mankind. And God is faithful; he will not let you be tempted beyond what you can bear. But when you are tempted, he will also provide a way out so that you can endure it (1 Corinthians 10:12-13).

Consider This:

When was the last time you played with temptation? What was it, and why did it entice you? Did it "bite" you? If so, how? Did you finally flee? If so, how has that helped? If not, would you confess it to the Lord right now and take the way of escape He provides?

Lessons from a Trilingual Cat
Communicate Love

There are hundreds of languages in the
world but a smile speaks them all.

AUTHOR UNKNOWN

Pokey is a "trilingual" cat that lives with my friend Pouri's family. He understands and responds to commands in three different languages. It wasn't something he planned to do. It just happened. His people are from Iran and speak both Farsi and English. Their housekeeper talks Spanish to the cat. Being rather smart, Pokey picked up key words in all three tongues. But it's doubtful he even knows he did it. To him, these sounds are probably just one language—"human speak." They are sounds that get him fed and petted and close to his people...and his desire to relate to them has spurred him to learn what they mean.

Pokey also has a language of his own that he has taught his humans. It's his own dialect of cat speak—a mix of meows and sign language. Pokey uses this to make his wishes and needs known, and it is very effective.

When Pokey wants the chicken he loves, he goes and sits by the fridge. When he wants kitty treats, he parks himself beneath the cupboard where they are kept. If he wants Pouri to give him her special kitty back rub with her flyswatter, he comes and stands under the cabinet where it's stored, looks up, and meows.

Pokey's responsiveness to his humans has endeared him to their hearts. So have his efforts to communicate with them. Love and care have overcome the language barrier and built bridges of understanding between cat and people.

Making an effort to "speak" to others with caring and cultural sensitivity can also build bridges that help in sharing God's love. Sadly, I fell short in this area as a new believer.

I am a Jewish believer in Jesus. I first came to know my Messiah when I was in college. But I was young and rebellious and more interested in asserting my own "rights" than in being sensitive to my family. When I spent several weeks with my parents the following summer, I did something that caused my mom real pain.

I decided I wanted to wear a symbol of my newfound faith—a cross. I knew this might bother my mom, but I didn't let that stop me. One day, I bought a cross pendant and put it on. I didn't say anything to my folks. But I'd left the jewelry box on a kitchen counter. Mom opened it, saw the indentation of the cross inside, and hit the proverbial roof. She told me I could wear that around my friends, but not in her house.

I snapped that she had no right to tell me what I could wear…period!

Some Jewish people find the symbol of the cross off-putting. They associate it with centuries of persecution by people who called themselves Christians but didn't show God's love to Jewish people. Mom's reaction was much more personal, however. Decades later, she told me she'd felt like a failure when I came to faith in Jesus. She must have felt she hadn't given me an adequate appreciation of the Jewish religion and my heritage. The cross around my neck screamed failure and dripped acid on that wound.

Ultimately, I appeased my mom while still having my way by wearing a cross, a Jewish star, and a mustard seed all on the same chain. But my heart was wrong and my witness fell flat. I was refusing to speak the most vital language of all—the language of love! Fortunately, I learned better over the decades since, and I believe Mom did indeed come to know her Messiah before her death at age 91.

Since Mom's passing, God has tugged at my heart to become more familiar with the cultural language of my Jewish roots. I host a Messianic Bible study in my home. We have group prayer standing and facing toward Jerusalem. We recite Old Testament prayers in English and in Hebrew. We had Hanukkah, Purim, and Passover celebrations. And we're discussing the New Testament Book of Acts in a "cultural language" that embraces a Jewish context. We've talked about how these early first century believers in Messiah were considered a sect of Judaism. We've looked at how they began to create a whole new and different kind of Messianic community. In a completely different way— culturally rather than physically—we are doing what the Holy Spirit did at Pentecost (Acts 2). We are translating the gospel into the "native tongue" of those we desire to hear its message.

It is interesting that the Pentecost event constitutes a symbolic reversal of a much earlier divine intervention in language. Genesis 11:1 tells us that at one time, "the whole world had one language and a common speech." But the people became disobedient and prideful. After the flood, God had told them to spread out and populate the whole earth. But they wanted to come together and build a city and a high tower to the heavens—the Tower of Babel. God was not pleased. In Genesis 11:6-7 we read, "The LORD said, 'If as one people speaking the same language they have begun to do this, then nothing they plan to do will be impossible for them. Come, let us go down and confuse their language so they will not understand each other.'" Man had tried to use common language as an aid to evil. Now, at Pentecost, God was using language as a means of spreading the good news of His redemptive plan for the ages.

Pokey the cat learned other languages so he could communicate with those he cared about. We need to do the same. What better way to break down barriers of misunderstanding and build bridges over which God's love can flow?

All of them were filled with the Holy Spirit and began to speak in other tongues as the Spirit enabled them (Acts 2:4).

Consider This:

How has physical or cultural language been a barrier in sharing your faith? How has it been a bridge? Is there someone whose "cultural language" you could learn better as an aid in sharing God's love? In what other ways might you "speak" love and caring to others?

Saving Mr. Sinj
God's Ways Aren't Ours

God moves in a mysterious way
His wonders to perform;
He plants His footsteps in the sea
And rides upon the storm.

WILLIAM COWPER

Susu loved animals, but her dad was allergic and didn't allow them in the house. Then, when she was still a young girl, her dad left the family. Susu decided that her mom needed a pet, so she brought home a sweet little puppy she named Molly. At first, her mom didn't think this was such a good idea, but in time she and Molly became great friends.

Time passed. Susu decided her mom could use a kitty too. She chose a teeny too-small-to-be-weaned kitten someone had found in the back of a pickup truck. He had been abandoned and left to die. But Susu thought he was just perfect. She put him in a picnic basket with a bow and gave it to her mom as a surprise birthday present. Her mom wasn't as excited as Susu had hoped when she saw this darling but very sick ball of orange and white fur. They took him to the vet and didn't get an optimistic prognosis. The vet wasn't even sure the kitten would make it through the first night.

Susu remembers praying that God would keep the little guy alive for her mom—because even if her mom didn't know it yet, a kitten was just what she needed. They made the kitty a comfortable bed, petted him for a while, and went to relax in the den. When they came back to check on him before heading off to sleep, they couldn't find him anywhere. Then Susu heard her dog Molly barking. She found Molly lying on her side. The kitten was nestled in the fur on her belly, all snug and warm. Needless to say, he survived after all. He got healthier and stronger with each hour. But he didn't have a name yet. He was just "that little kitten."

Susu kept praying every night for the kitty to make it. Every morning she'd find him right where she left him, snuggled into Molly's warm furry belly. Then one morning she went to get him and he wasn't there. Susu and her mom looked everywhere. They got everyone else in their household searching, even the dog. Still no kitten! Suddenly, her mom remembered she had put some water on the stove to boil so she could make tea. As they headed to the kitchen, they smelled something burning. They found the kitten happily keeping warm on the stove. But he hadn't realized yet that his fur was burning! It was black and curled, and so were his whiskers. They put him in the sink, drenched him with water, and wrapped him in a towel. From that moment, Susu's mom started getting attached to the little fellow. She even gave him a name—Mr. Sinj.

In retrospect, it may not have been the brightest idea to give such a small, sickly kitten as a gift. But Susu's heart was right, and God works in unexpected ways. He used a dog to nurture the kitten, and a fire to warm and change Susu's mom's heart so she began to embrace her new pet. Susu moved to California after college and took Molly with her. Mr. Sinj remained with her mom and they stayed close and shared life together for 15 years.

God has also met my needs in ways I might not have chosen. When I was a freshman in college I traveled with the ladies' choir doing concerts up and down the state of California. It was springtime and the weather was great when we left southern California, so I didn't think of taking a coat. Northern California was a different story. One night it was cold and raining and I was miserable. A sweet young girl offered to give me her old worn-out navy peacoat. It was huge and I thought it quite ugly, but I gratefully accepted. It warmed me like a nice big hug from an old friend. I was more of a flowery fashion girl and this was a heavy navy blue coat—not what I would have chosen. But I learned to love the look of it. I thought of how patriotic it was to wear such a garment, and I felt proud to have it on. I wore it several times during the tour, and for years afterwards, and I was thankful to have it.

When Jesus walked this earth, He didn't do things like we do either. He chose a tax collector named Matthew to be one of His disciples. Jews of that day looked at tax collectors as sinners and cheats who sold out to Rome. The religious elite would never have picked such a fellow for that type of position. But God's ways aren't ours. He knew that Matthew was ready to respond and repent. Matthew turned from his former ways to faithfully follow the Lord and even wrote a book of the New Testament that still bears his name.

God's methods are often different from ours. He uses "foolish" people to confound the worldly-wise. He uses sickly cats to comfort lonely moms, old, "ugly" coats to warm cold bodies, and sin-sick humans to share His message of redemption with the world. His ways and thoughts may not be ours, but they are always wisest and best!

"For my thoughts are not your thoughts, neither are your ways my ways," declares the LORD. "As the heavens are higher than the earth, so are my ways higher than your ways and my thoughts than your thoughts" (Isaiah 55:8-9).

Consider This:

Has God ever worked in your life in a way you would not have chosen? How did you respond? Looking back, how were God's ways better and wiser? How has this built your faith and trust in Him?

And He Lived to Meow Again
Don't Miss God's Grace

*How many times do we miss God's blessings
because they are not packaged as we expected?*

Even the old adage of a cat having nine lives doesn't adequately explain the miraculous saga of Lyndon. He lived in a 13th floor apartment in the Bronx, New York. My cousin's husband Jim was part of the family that owned him and he still recalls the day Lyndon could have gone to his final reward.

The family was on their balcony. It had some fencing but there were breaks in the protective mesh. Lyndon got out on the balcony, breached the fence and toppled 13 stories down. (Such an incident highlights the hazards of a cat being on a balcony even under supervision, regardless of precautions taken. Falling from short heights can also have serious consequences for a feline.)

Lyndon's family feared the worst. But when they went downstairs, to their amazement and relief, they found their cat hiding in the bushes, very much alive. Except for a tiny scratch, he was none the worse for his misadventure.

Living through one such experience is amazing enough. But Jim suspects that Lyndon gave an encore. Sometime after that first incident, he was found outside on the street by a neighbor. People in the building knew Lyndon and Jim thinks it highly unlikely he could have made his way down the elevator and out the door without being intercepted. The most likely explanation is that Lyndon took a second tumble off the balcony—and survived that too.

Did Lyndon know how lucky he was? Did it ever enter his furry head that he might be a living, breathing, four-footed feline miracle? Almost certainly not. After all, he was a cat! But we humans also sometimes miss God's miracles of grace in our lives. Or we look at the negative side of a situation instead of seeing God's hand of blessing—as I did one recent Christmas season.

My friend Cindy often helps me decorate my home for the holidays. On this December afternoon, she was piling boxes of Christmas things on a large glass living room coffee table. I was in an adjoining room when I was startled by a horrific noise. I rushed in—and discovered my table had crashed.

This was no ordinary coffee table. It was an art glass statement. Fused glass of various shapes and textures made up the large, heavy, square tabletop. Additional decorative glass pieces were glued to its underside. This giant slab of glass was supported by a pedestal made of three separate glass pieces, also in varying shapes. We deduced later that one of those pedestal pieces had weakened, unbeknownst to me, and had given way without warning. The table's top had slid sideways and crashed to the ground, breaking into large, jagged chunks.

My first unholy reaction was to rail against God. How could He let this happen, and of all times, now? This was a custom coffee table, a centerpiece of the room, and not easily or quickly replaced. In just a few days I was having a party. What was I going to do?

Cindy gently corrected my myopic spiritual vision. She pointed out the miracle I'd missed. She let me know that instead of grumbling, I ought to praise and thank God. That table could have crashed at any time. What if a whole group of people had been gathered around it—as had happened just days earlier, at Thanksgiving? What if some of them had been badly hurt? What if a jagged spear of glass had impaled her leg and caused serious harm? She had in fact gotten cut by the glass, but suffered only mild scratches.

My friend's words forced me to refocus. She was right! In my selfishness, I had missed God's grace. Once I stopped grousing and repented, God opened the way for me to borrow a coffee table to get me through the holidays and beyond. I also made sure my next table was tempered glass. I'd never even realized the old one wasn't, and could be a potential lethal weapon if it broke.

God did many signs and wonders so Moses could lead His people out of Egypt. But when the Egyptians pursued them, they balked. "It would have been better for us to serve the Egyptians than to die in the desert!" they groaned (Exodus 14:12). They failed to see they were in the midst of a miracle of deliverance. But Moses saw, and urged them to trust. Sure enough, God parted the Red Sea for them and drowned their enemies.

Lyndon was blind to his miracle of grace. So was I, until Cindy helped me see. Are your spiritual eyes in or out of focus? I believe God is constantly at work in our lives in amazing ways. If we watch for His miracles and thank and praise Him, it will bless our lives and grow our faith.

He performs wonders that cannot be fathomed, miracles that cannot be counted (Job 9:10).

Consider This:

What are some ways God has shown you grace? What small miracles have you seen Him do for you or loved ones? Did you ever miss a miracle at first, but see it later? How can you sharpen your spiritual vision for the future?

Purr-fect Freedom
God Frees Us to Be His

Just living is not enough...One must have sunshine, freedom, and a little flower.

HANS CHRISTIAN ANDERSEN

Midnight, you know you don't belong on that table!" I exclaimed. For a week now my little black cat had been acting like a wild woman, despite being over 13 years of age. She'd been running at high speed over the furniture, playing as hard as she had in her youth. She'd batted at the living room curtain pulls for nearly half an hour. She'd even tried to pick fights with her feline younger brother, Mooch, just for something to do. Yesterday she'd shadowed me constantly. The day before she'd wracked my nerves as she weaved in and out of the second story banister the way she had when she was very young. Back then she'd once fallen down to the first floor. Thankfully, she wasn't hurt. We feared it might happen again—with far worse results.

What had gotten into Midnight? She'd even perched on the coffee table, bobbing her head up and down and leaping at the images on the TV screen when we were watching the Olympic snowboarding competition. Why was she acting so strange?

Then it hit us. She was "out of jail." My daughter's family, who lives with us, had gone on vacation, taking their two toddler boys with them. Midnight no longer felt caged in by children who watched her every move. She could play without danger of any interference from the little ones. She was delighted. She was celebrating. She was free at last!

I knew just how Midnight felt. In a whole different way, I was recently surprised by a "get out of jail" card too. My husband Phil had surgery and was in the hospital. Phil is prone to forming blood clots and is on blood-thinning medication. They had taken him off it for the operation. Now his blood had to be quickly thinned again. Since he was ready to come home, it fell to me to give him the necessary shots twice a day in his belly. The nurse taught me how to do this and gave me a pep talk about how easy it was. I thought, "Yes, but you're a nurse and I'm a wimp!" They sent us home with a prescription for ten needles filled with the medicine. I tried to pump myself up, but internally I was dreading giving each of those injections.

I've had to give Phil such shots before, so it wasn't that the task was new. I just hated having to hurt Phil, or even think of that possibility. I remember quoting the verse "I can do all things through Him who strengthens me" (Philippians 4:13, NASB) for hours before I gave him his first injection. He was wonderful about it, even though I left bruises and made him wince.

I set the time schedule for the shots securely in my mind and wished I could fast forward to next week. I delivered three shots successfully. The fourth injection closely coincided with Phil's doctor's appointment, so I brought the needle along. I planned to beg the doctor or nurse to do it for me this one time. After the doctor tested Phil's blood, he gave me the most wonderful news I could have imagined. He said I wouldn't need to give Phil any more shots because the injections he'd already gotten had brought his blood back to a safe level.

I left that office floating on air. As I drove Phil home I began to sing. I felt light, happy and full of energy—just like Midnight must have. I was free! I felt released. And in my heart I was racing across the curtains for joy.

Freedom is defined as the power or right to act or speak as one wants without hindrance or restraint. That was the gift both Midnight and I were given. She was freed from rambunctious toddlers who intruded on her space and I was freed from a task I dreaded to perform.

Freedom is also a biblical concept. In Galatians 5:1, Paul wrote: "It is for freedom that Christ has set us free. Stand firm, then, and do not let yourselves be burdened again by a yoke of slavery." What did he mean by this?

The churches of Galatia included many Jews who had found their Messiah. They had once thought that to gain right standing before a holy God, they must keep the Jewish law. Now they'd been taught that faith in Jesus' death for their sins on the cross was what saved them. They heard that they must trust His works, not their own. They could not work their way to God no matter how hard they tried. But if they believed in Jesus their Messiah, they would receive salvation as God's free gift. This was the ultimate "get out of jail free" card!

However, false prophets had come to Galatia and were contradicting this truth. They were telling these Jewish believers that they must go back to keeping all the rules and regulations—or they weren't saved. Paul wrote to urge them not to relinquish the freedom they had been given. Trying to earn their salvation meant returning to bondage. They needed to embrace their new freedom in Christ and learn to walk in it.

Freedom in Christ is a wonderful thing because it frees us to live for God out of gratitude rather than fear. It also frees us from pride by showing us we can't ever earn our own forgiveness. And it frees us to be what God desires—a grateful people who recognize what He has done for us so that joy springs out of our hearts.

Freedom put a kitten-like spring in Midnight's step as she raced around the house, and it lifted a burden from me. God's "purr-fect" freedom puts a song in every heart that knows Jesus. God longs for His people to live in His freedom every day. Have you experienced it yet?

Therefore, there is now no condemnation for those who are in Christ Jesus, because through Christ Jesus the law of the Spirit who gives life has set you free from the law

of sin and death. For what the law was powerless to do because it was weakened by the flesh, God did by sending his own Son in the likeness of sinful flesh to be a sin offering (Romans 8:1-3).

Consider This:

When was the last time you felt real freedom in your life? Have you received God's gift of freedom through faith in Jesus? If not, will you ask Him to forgive your sins and come into your life right now?

Lost Next Door

Let God Lead You Home

*I have never been lost, but I will admit
to being confused for several weeks.*

Daniel Boone

I would never have learned about Girlie and Grey Boy being lost kitties had it not been for my friend Cindy. It was evening. We'd been to dinner and had just driven back to my home. We both saw the man and child, but I wasn't in an outreaching mood. I was still grieving a loss of my own: my beloved sheltie mix, Morgan, had vanished from my yard just weeks before. I wasn't into talking with people and learning their stories. But Cindy realized something might be wrong and took time to speak with the dad and daughter.

Thanks to her caring, we found out that this neighbor's beloved family cats had slipped out when a door was accidentally left open. They were indoor kitties and likely couldn't find their own way home. Father and daughter were out searching for them, but had had no luck. I got their email and the cats' description so I could make contact in case I happened to catch a glimpse of the missing four-foots.

I take an hour-long walk in my neighborhood every day. Part of my walk is on this family's street. Next afternoon as I headed that way, I prayed. Tender from my own loss, I asked God if He might allow me to see one of their missing cats. And as I turned down their street, I did indeed see a Siamese-type kitty on the opposite side of the block. It fit my neighbors' description of Girlie. I debated trying to approach it. When I did, the kitty took off.

I wasn't sure of my neighbors' house number. Racing home I found their email, but there was no street address. I sent my neighbors an email alert, then headed back to their street and knocked on some doors, hoping someone would know where they lived. The best I could uncover was one person's guess as to which house might belong to the kitties' owners.

Then, as I trudged back up the block on the side where I'd seen the possible truant, a car pulled up. A mom and two young girls got out. One of them looked like the child from the night before. I hurried over and we confirmed that this was indeed the family. When they heard the description, they were certain I'd spied Girlie…only a house or two away from where they lived.

I continued on with my walk and left them to follow through on my lead. Later that day I got an email from the very grateful father. They'd found Girlie at the house next door, and searching further, had discovered Grey Boy hiding under the very same home. Their kitties had been oh so close—and yet so far because they hadn't a clue about how to find their way back to their people.

It's not only kitties that can get "lost next door." Decades ago I visited Munich with my mother. I went off shopping on my own, got turned around, and couldn't find my way back to my hotel. I tried to ask directions, but for whatever reason, no one I stopped that day spoke enough English to help me. I knew I wasn't that far away, but "closeness" did me no more good than it would do Girlie and Grey Boy all those years later. Fortunately, I had written the name and address of my hotel on a slip of paper. I hailed a cab and gave the driver the information. In a few minutes I was safely "home."

We can also be lost next door in a spiritual sense. That's what happened to a young man I'll call Juan. Juan lived with relatives. One of them was involved in a Christian ministry, often spoke in churches, and had taken Juan along on these engagements for years.

Recently Juan, who is now 18, came to visit my Community Bible Study class. This class is part of an international ministry to encourage people to study God's Word. Juan's neighbor, Nic, is part of our class and took an interest in the young man. He brought Juan and got him to sign up for a full course of study beginning next fall. As Nic was helping him register, he asked Juan's level of Bible knowledge. Nic figured it was probably medium. He was shocked when Juan said none. Juan explained that though he'd gone with his relative to churches for all those years, he had never really listened to the Bible teaching.

I don't know if Juan has a personal relationship with the Lord. Even if he does, he has been "lost next door" when it comes to probing the riches of what that relationship involves and how it can bless his life. But, he's anxious to be "found" by digging into God's Word and learning more about what it says.

Our loving Lord cares deeply for all who are lost, including those "lost next door." One of these was a Pharisee named Nicodemus. Jesus explained that "no one can enter the kingdom of God unless he is born of water and the Spirit" (John 3:5). Nicodemus didn't get it. "'You are Israel's teacher,' said Jesus, 'and do you not understand these things?'" (John 3:10). Jesus went on to explain the new birth, and although Nicodemus didn't fully comprehend it then, he eventually came to faith.

Girlie and Grey Boy needed help to get home. So does Juan, and so might someone in your life. Will you be watching for those "lost next door" who God might be nudging you to reach out to and lead back home to Him?

In the same way your Father in heaven is not willing that any of these little ones should perish (Matthew 18:14).

Consider This:

What are some ways that people you know might be lost next door? How might you reach out to them? Is it possible you might be going through the motions of the Christian life and yet not experiencing its depth? If so, is there a Bible study class you might join that would help you deepen your relationship with the Lord?

Queenie for a Day
Is Your Royalty Outward or Inward?

A throne is only a bench covered with velvet.

NAPOLEON BONAPARTE

Phil and Erin couldn't think of a better name for their precious new little white Persian kitty than Queen Felina. They gave "Queenie" a beautiful pillow of her own in the den—a throne where she could preside over all her new subjects and be entertained by them. Sophie, their 14-year-old daughter, made the kitty a special crown. Queenie was given a food dish and collar with her name printed on them. Even her cat box was special. Erin found a lovely pink one with little gold crowns decorating the edges. It didn't take Queenie very long to believe she was royalty—until the day she went too far.

On this particular evening, Queenie tried to claim a new throne of her own choosing. Phil came home and went straight to his favorite chair to sit and relax after a hard day's work. Queenie had gotten there first. When he tried to shoo her off, she growled and swiped at him. He was not about to let her reign over him in this fashion, so he picked her up and put her out in the backyard.

Queen Felina had been dethroned! She lay by the back door and glared through the window at Phil. He was too tired to notice. After a while, they both relaxed and calmed down. Phil invited Queenie back in. Rather than prancing around as she was known to do, she walked slowly and deliberately into the den, sat on her pillow, and didn't bother anyone for the rest of the evening.

Queenie never tried to usurp Phil's throne again. She had learned her place. They remained friends for the rest of her life.

Queenie the cat had to learn that the outward trappings of royalty didn't mean she could call the shots with her humans. She was a little less royal than she thought. On at least one occasion, our great-niece, Nikki, proved herself to be more royal than we ever dreamed!

Nikki had been entered in a beauty pageant for little girls. She was only four years old at the time, and she'd had no formal training. Yet, Nikki took her place on the stage and walked its length and back with the confidence and grace of a little princess. That day, she was awarded four trophies…for looks, smile, poise, and talent. We were blown away! Nikki was truly royal!

Those who have a personal relationship with Jesus are royalty in an even deeper and more special way. If we learn what it means to be God's child and live that out, our royalty will shine through regardless of our outward appearance or circumstances. When I was young, I had a mentor who I thought of as royalty. She was very poor in material things, but ever so rich and regal in her sweet and joyful spirit. She was not beautiful as the world sees beauty, but her wonderfully weathered face was always lit up by a sweet, peaceful smile. When I decided to sell greeting cards as a child, she gave me wonderful advice. She said my face was what people would remember. She told me I should reflect Jesus with my face and my smile. She said kindness is what sells best if it is true and loving. I always smile when I remember that kind woman who loved her Lord and wanted to please Him.

Scripture is filled with examples of royalty. Many of Israel's kings had the outward trappings, like Queenie, but did not have a heart for God and did evil in His sight. David had the heart God was looking for—a heart after God's own—and was chosen to be Israel's next king when he was just a shepherd boy. There were times when he strayed from God and sinned, but he always turned back and repented and sought to follow the Lord. And it is through David's line that Jesus our Messiah was born.

When He lived among us, Jesus didn't look like royalty outwardly. Isaiah wrote, "He had no beauty or majesty to attract us to him, nothing in his appearance that we should desire him. He was despised and rejected by mankind, a man of suffering, and familiar with pain. Like one from whom men hide their faces he was despised, and we held him in low esteem" (Isaiah 53:2-3). Yet this is the One of whom Paul wrote, "God exalted him to the highest place and gave him the name that is above every name, that at the name of Jesus every knee should bow, in heaven and on earth and under the earth, and every tongue acknowledge that Jesus Christ is Lord, to the glory of God the Father" (Philippians 2:9-11).

Jesus calls us to be royal inside—to be His royal priesthood, ministering in His name with humility and love. My mentor did this, and that's why I thought of her as a queen. I'm not sure she would have agreed, but I think Jesus would. I think He is pleased with her and all who are royal in Him with a royalty that will never fade, but will reflect His glory forever!

But you are a chosen people, a royal priesthood, a holy nation, God's special possession, that you may declare the praises of him who called you out of darkness into his wonderful light (1 Peter 2:9).

Consider This:

Who would you consider "royalty" in your life? What makes them royal to you? Do you believe God sees them that way as well? Why or why not? Are you a member of God's royal priesthood? If not, what is holding you back? If so, how might you reflect His royalty even more to others?

A Creature Called Dog
Fear Blocks Friendship

*Our doubts are traitors, and make us lose the
good we oft might win, by fearing to attempt.*

WILLIAM SHAKESPEARE

I would have loved a dog growing up, but my parents weren't big on
indoor pets. Cats, however, could live outside. I got my first pair at
age nine. Except for very brief intervals, I've had kitties ever since. I
didn't give up my dog dreams, but I felt that to have a pup I needed a
house with a yard and a job that allowed me to be home enough so the
pooch didn't feel like an orphan. Those planets finally converged about
16 years ago.

At that point I had two kitties, Barney and Misty. They ruled the
roost. They had never lived with a creature called "dog." When I
brought home a fluffy white bundle of puppy joy named Biscuit, she
was anything but a joy to them!

Biscuit was spring-loaded with energy, and she loved chasing my
poor kitties. She wasn't being aggressive or mean—she was playing. But
they didn't understand this, and they spent the next five months of their
lives staying as high and far away from their new four-footed family
member as they could get. In my home that meant leaping atop kitchen

counters where my rambunctious puppy couldn't follow. It took from August to New Year's Day until one of my cats would stay on the same couch with Biscuit for more than a heartbeat. My chocolate brown boy, Barney, eventually came to terms with the situation. My little grey and white female, Misty, had a tougher time. Biscuit knew she could chase Misty and get a rise out of her. This was way too much fun for a puppy to resist, and Misty's own fears prolonged her misery. Misty did learn, though, that I could control her tormentor, and she was braver when I took command and called Biscuit off.

Looking back on the formation of my animal family, I can see how fear blocked friendship. How could my kitties learn my puppy was safe to be around if they wouldn't get close enough to find out? Fear prevented them from getting the face time they needed to get comfortable with Biscuit—at least at first.

The same thing can happen in human relationships.

I am from a Jewish background. In my junior year of college, I met a species of Christian I had not yet encountered. I had just transferred to a new school. A student in my dorm began to talk to me about having a personal relationship with God. She invited me to visit a Bible study she and some other students attended once a week in a dining hall on campus. I had been on a personal spiritual search for years, and also wanted to meet people in my new school. I went.

Though not as leery as Barney and Misty would be of Biscuit all those years later, I was somewhat skittish. If these students had "chased" me, I probably would have run away. But they were gentle and accepting. They didn't push or pressure me. They just answered my questions and showed me unconditional love. Eventually one of them asked to read through a tract with me that explained we have all sinned and fallen short of God's standard of perfect holiness. It explained that Jesus (Yeshua) died to pay for our sins and bridge the gap between man and God. She invited me to pray and ask Jesus to come into my heart and be my Messiah, Savior and Lord. I said I wasn't ready to do that. She told me that was fine, and put the tract away. Because my new friends didn't pressure me, I didn't have to "go high" and avoid them like my cats did with Biscuit years later. I felt safe enough to keep attending the weekly meetings.

Time passed. I was intrigued with my new friends' faith, but I was struggling to believe that Jesus was God. One day, I shared this with my dorm friend. She suggested I ask God to show me if it was true. I couldn't think of anything more honest. She wasn't trying to twist my arm. She was just pointing out that if God was real, He would show me.

I prayed that prayer. God answered it. I was introduced to passages in the Psalms and Isaiah that showed me you could get to a belief in Jesus (Yeshua) through Old Testament Scriptures. I put my faith and trust in Him and have walked with Him for over four decades. Because I wasn't scared off, I not only made some marvelous new human friends, but I entered into friendship with my beloved Messiah.

Jesus is our ultimate Friend because He gave His life for us. He also acts to reassure us when our fear is hindering a deeper relationship with Him. That's what He did with the woman in Luke 8:43-48. She'd had a bleeding disorder for 12 years, and no one had been able to help her. She came behind Jesus in a crowd, touched His cloak, and was instantly healed. Jesus felt power go out and asked who had done this. At first, the woman kept silent. Only when she realized that she couldn't hide did she come forward and fall trembling before Him. She confessed what she'd done and why. And Jesus reached out in loving friendship to take their relationship to the next level, saying, "Daughter, your faith has healed you. Go in peace" (Luke 8:48).

Biscuit the dog didn't understand how her actions were putting my kitties off. But we as believers can share with care. We can learn to listen to God's Holy Spirit and reach out in ways that don't chase people off, but draw them into God's loving arms.

I have become all things to all people so that by all possible means I might save some (1 Corinthians 9:22).

Consider This:

Have people ever shared their faith in a way that made you want to "go high"? What could they have done to make you feel more comfortable with them? How might you stay more in tune with God's Spirit when you share so you don't inadvertently scare someone off?

See Sammy Run

Choose Healing

*The strongest principle of growth
lies in human choice.*

GEORGE ELIOT

Cindy first met Sammy late one night when she was driving home. As she was passing a large industrial building, she spied what looked like a cat in the middle of the road. She was tired. The last thing she wanted to do was go back and check. But she thought, "What if that kitty gets hit by a car?"

Cindy cares deeply for animals. That cat's image haunted her. Half a mile down the road, she turned her car around—and found an orange and white tabby sitting frozen in the street, seemingly unable to move. His eyes were wide, but she didn't see blood. Perhaps he'd been hit by a vehicle and was in shock. Cautiously, she reached to pick him up. He offered no resistance. She thought of taking him to an emergency vet, but she couldn't afford it. So she drove him to her house instead. She fixed up a crate with food and water, a litter pan, and a heating pad (to help with the possible shock), and put him inside.

Next day Cindy opened the crate and found a whole new Sammy.

He flew against the crate's back, hissing and snarling. He was clearly terrified, and fear had made him vicious. Cindy wondered if he'd warm up in time.

Sammy didn't. He reached through the crate and tried to get at Cindy. He was perilous to approach. She was forced to cut a piece of plywood and slide it into the crate at an angle to nudge Sammy into one corner so she could change the litter pan and keep him fed and watered.

Time passed. Cindy was caring for other cats on her desert property. She eventually built a cat run. She released Sammy into one sectioned-off, roofed corner of the structure. She'd been advised to ignore Sammy and not make eye contact with him. She kept him in the run, provided for his needs, and waited. It took about a year, but finally Sammy started purring when Cindy came in—as long as their eyes didn't meet. If she made eye contact, he hissed and fled.

Sammy had built a wall of fear. Cindy countered with a commitment of love. She would not abandon Sammy. She would not set time limits on her love and care for him. She would keep being there for him on whatever level he would allow—indefinitely.

Recently, Sammy escaped from the cat run. But Cindy's property is fenced, and he's still within its bounds. She got a doghouse for him. He goes in to eat. She could and would protect him better—but he won't permit it. Will he, in time? "Purr-haps"—or "purr-haps" not!

Like Sammy, we humans may throw up fear walls that block our healing. We may make choices that don't let others help us. Cindy's sister Carrie did this for decades. But eventually, she chose to respond to love, and it turned her life around.

Growing up, Carrie was easily frustrated. She found it hard to push through problems. Her parents split. There were family difficulties. Carrie slipped into drugs.

Periodically, Carrie's father tried to help. Once he bought her a little VW Beetle. She didn't maintain it, blew the engine, and left it on the side of the road. Another time he helped her with rent—but eventually she got evicted anyway.

Carrie felt like a failure. She started avoiding her dad so she didn't have to lie and sneak away to get the drugs she craved. She desperately wanted to change. She wanted a different life. She wanted her father's love and approval. But she didn't know how to get there. She knew he was a man of high standards, and she feared she couldn't measure up.

God knew what Carrie didn't—that with Him all things are possible and while she had breath, it was not too late for her.

When Carrie was in her fifties, her father was diagnosed with cancer. Other family members helped care for him. But at a certain point in time, a "care gap" occurred, and they asked Carrie to help. Faced with his mortality, her father had embraced a personal relationship with Jesus Christ. He understood unconditional love as never before. He told Carrie he cared for her and asked how he might help her get her life straightened out.

Love and acceptance from her earthly father filled a hole in Carrie. She was ready to let him—and God—help her. She started on a journey of healing that involved costly accountability. She even served a few months of jail time. She entered rehab. She reported to a probation officer. Her father passed away, but her sister, my friend Cindy, offered love and support. Unlike Sammy, Carrie chose to take down her fear wall and let help and healing in.

Carrie's battle is ongoing—as is each of our battles against the old demons that would drag us down. But, as I write this, she is conquering them in Christ. Only once did she slip and take drugs. When it happened, she went to her probation officer, confessed, and sought his help in getting back on track. On a deeper level, she leans on God every day to sustain her, and gets her grown children and grandchildren praying about everything!

God's heart is to heal and restore. But sometimes we act like Sammy and don't allow it. The Israelites of old didn't always respond to God either. But He kept reaching out. In 2 Chronicles 7:14, God said: "If my people, who are called by my name, will humble themselves and pray and seek my face and turn from their wicked ways, then I will hear from heaven, and I will forgive their sin and will heal their land."

Sammy doesn't realize he's blocking the healing and blessing his human could give. He's a cat. He reacts out of instinct. We humans have a much more conscious choice. Like Carrie, we all have areas of our lives that our loving heavenly Father wants to heal—if we would permit Him. Will you choose to hiss and flee? Or will you purr and let Him lift you into His arms and make you whole?

Lord my God, I called to you for help, and you healed me (Psalm 30:2).

Consider This:

Have you ever made fear-based choices that blocked God and others from helping you heal? What were they? What was the result? Are you permitting healing now? If not, why not? If so, how has it changed your life?

Simba Tops It Off
Only God Can Fill Us Up

*You can never get enough of what you
don't need to make you happy.*

ERIC HOFFER

Patti had a skinny cat named Simba who loved to eat. As a matter of fact, she would eat anything and everything. Her human family had to be vigilant in monitoring her because she seemed to have an antenna for food, and rather than stopping when she was full she would top off her tummy just like people top off their gas tanks.

One Thanksgiving, as Patti and her mom were preparing the huge meal, they left the cooked turkey and the delicious gravy on the counter for just a few minutes so they could catch the beginning of the Macy's Thanksgiving Day Parade.

When they returned they found that Simba had "topped off her tank" to an alarming degree. She had totally emptied the gravy bowl and licked it clean. Simba looked pregnant because her belly was so full. Unable to walk, she just sat there, motionless, her face smeared with grease. Patti's dad was so alarmed by the sight of Simba's belly that he rushed to the phone to call a friend who was knowledgeable about cats. The man said either their kitty would die or recover. Thankfully, she survived. The next morning Simba was mobile again…and ready to eat once more.

Simba's treasure was in food, but she could never get enough. Stuffing herself never satisfied her. Being a cat, she couldn't analyze her actions and realize this. Unlike Simba, we humans are able to reflect on our choices and their consequences. But we don't always do so until a crisis arises.

That was the case with Janice, a friend of mine who lost herself in shopping. It was the time in America when credit cards were easy to get. She was thrilled each time one arrived in her mail slot. She called the number to activate the card and didn't hesitate to use it. Janice had over 15 credit cards within a year! However, she also had over 15 bills to be paid. Her husband realized they were in terrible trouble and feared her excesses would ruin their finances. He talked about it with Janice, but that didn't get her to stop. He tried suggesting she limit the use of her cards, but that didn't work. Next, he demanded that she give up half of them, but that only meant she maxed out the rest. Finally, he did the unthinkable: when she was sleeping one night he found and destroyed all her cards. He knew she would keep on "topping off her tank" otherwise. He was worried his action would end the marriage, but instead it forced her to see the reality she had created.

Janice and her husband began the difficult process of paying off their debts. She learned to be content with a designated amount of cash to spend. Their marriage actually became stronger as a result. Janice was trying to fill a hole by "topping off" with things the way Simba did with food. But she found out that only God could truly fill her up. She used the crisis to draw closer to Him and her hunger to shop dissipated.

Whether it's Simba with food or Janice with credit cards, God is not pleased when we gorge on the things of this world. Jesus was asked to help out in a dispute between brothers about an inheritance. He said to both of them, "Watch out! Be on your guard against all kinds of greed; life does not consist in an abundance of possessions" (Luke 12:15). Simba's treasure was in food. She filled up on it at any cost, and may have put her life at risk. Janice's treasure was in shopping, and she almost ruined her marriage. The quarreling brothers' treasure was in an inheritance, and they let it come between them. Each time we try to fill ourselves up with anything other than the Lord, we are in danger of robbing ourselves of the greatest treasure of all.

Do not be afraid, little flock, for your Father has been pleased to give you the kingdom. Sell your possessions and give to the poor. Provide purses for yourselves that will not wear out, a treasure in heaven that will never fail, where no thief comes near and no moth destroys. For where your treasure is, there your heart will be also (Luke 12:32-34).

Consider This:

Are you satisfied with what you have, or do you always want more? How has that affected you? Do you treasure God above all else? If not, what are you "topping off" with? If so, how has God filled you?

Part V

Hiding in God's Protection

 MOOCH

Running Scared
Seek Refuge in God

You can't run away from trouble.
There ain't no place that far.

James Baskett as Uncle Remus

Thursday is when we roll all four of our trash cans out to the street for Friday garbage pickup. Our grandson Eli loves to help. We had just put the third out and turned to retrieve the last when I noticed Mooch sitting just outside the gate. He is our "friendly" cat. He loves following us around wherever we are. Since we were out front so was he, watching all the activity.

I had no sooner seen Mooch than I spied a flash of white running toward him. It was Juno, a big all-white Husky who visits our neighborhood almost daily. He is a nice dog, but he is feisty—and he is fast! Suddenly the trash cans were not the focus as Juno's owner raced over to get him. She and I are good friends who chat as often as we can, but at this time we were both frantically screaming women trying to stop what we both feared was to happen.

Mooch saw the danger, turned tail, and fled into the backyard for safety. That was good, but the gate was still open and Juno followed him. We had a car in the driveway, and Mooch began to race around it, closely trailed by Juno—nose to the ground to track Mooch by his scent. We two women were still screaming—not because it was the best way to get Juno's attention, but because we couldn't help it. Finally, as Mooch rounded the car once more, he spotted me and ran to me for help. I doubt I could have grabbed him in time, but at that exact moment, Juno's owner seized his collar and dragged him outside the gate. I rushed to close it. By now the neighbors were gathering to see what was wrong—but thankfully, the disaster had been avoided.

As I said a prayer of thanksgiving and headed inside with my cat, the thought crossed my mind that most of us humans react just like Mooch did when crisis hits. Our first impulse is to run in circles trying to get away from the trouble. There are many ways we do this. Such coping mechanisms work no better than Mooch running circles around the car. Even after all the running, the problem is still right there.

I reacted just like Mooch the night my husband had a stroke. Phil was in intensive care, recovering from heart bypass surgery. I'd gone home for a break when I got an urgent phone call from my son-in-law. "Phil's having a stroke! You need to come right away," he told me.

I literally began to run in circles in my living room. Like Mooch, I was in a state of panic. I had no rational thoughts. I was frantic. Then I thought about Jesus. I ran to Him spiritually. I cried out to Him with the most effective prayer of all: "Jesus…*help me!*" He answered, putting people's names in my mind to call. As I phoned each one, God put another name in my head. By the time I'd finished, one friend had pulled up out front to drive me to the hospital.

Panicking and running in circles didn't help, but once I ran to Jesus, He provided everything I needed. A dear friend was taking me to Phil. Others were on their way to join us. Still more were faithfully praying. I got to the hospital just in time to ride with Phil in an ambulance to UCLA's stroke center. What if I hadn't run to Jesus? I might have missed the transport and the support of those precious friends who came to the hospital to help us. As it turned out, before they did any surgery, God answered the prayers by dissolving the clot in Phil's brain, so the disaster was abated by the hand of God.

Many centuries ago, Jesus' disciples learned what a difference it could make to run to Him when disaster struck. They were crossing the Sea of Galilee with Jesus in a boat when they got caught in a terrible storm. We read in Mark 4:37 that "A furious squall came up, and the waves broke over the boat, so that it was nearly swamped." Jesus was sleeping when this horror happened, and the storm itself didn't rouse Him. But the disciples ran and woke Him in a panic. He commanded the storm to calm down, and it did. Their lives were spared and they learned just how powerful Jesus was. They asked each other, "Who is this? Even the wind and the waves obey him!" (Mark 4:41).

We believers understand that Jesus was God in human flesh, but the disciples were just learning that. Since His resurrection, He never sleeps (Psalm 121:4). We can run to Him just as Mooch ran to me and find shelter in any storm, at any time.

So, when trouble hits and you're tempted to panic, don't run in circles like Mooch and I did. Remember the disciples' experience in that squall. It was in a time of crisis that they learned just how powerful and present Jesus was! It's the same in our lives. It's the times when we feel like a huge beast is chasing us to tear us apart that the opportunities to grow in faith are greatest. If we run to Jesus for help, He will not let us down. At times, He may calm the outward storm. At other times, He may take us through it while calming the emotional storm inside. Either way, we will see more clearly that it is to Him we must run in danger, because He is our refuge and help.

God is our refuge and strength, an ever-present help in trouble. Therefore we will not fear, though the earth give way and the mountains fall into the heart of the sea, though its waters roar and foam and the mountains quake with their surging (Psalm 46:1-3).

Consider This:

What is your default response when trouble hits? How has it helped or hindered you in dealing with crisis? Have you called on Jesus for help? If so, what was the result? If not, next time you're tempted to run in circles, will you run to Him?

Why a Squeaky Cat Didn't Get the Grease

Is Your "Spiritual Manhole Cover" in Place?

The best armor is to keep out of range.

ITALIAN PROVERB

Squeak was a tiny orphan kitten when he joined my swim coach Matt's family. A little girl found him at the park on her way to school one morning. He was orange with green eyes and looked to be no more than six weeks old. She picked him up, took him with her to class, and called her parents to plead for permission to keep him. They said no. Then Matt's mom, who worked at the school, picked him up and held him for a while. As she held him, he grabbed her heart. That night Squeak became a member of Coach Matt's family. He was so tiny that Squeak seemed the appropriate name. His meow wasn't much more than a squeak either.

Over time, Squeak has lived up to his name in another way as well. When I think of a squeak, it can be either amusing or annoying. When our son John was just a little guy, he would get so excited about going fishing with his dad that he would wiggle in his chair and squeak with excitement. It was wonderful and it made us all laugh. On the other hand, have you ever had to push a squeaky grocery cart around the store? Or worse, have you had an unwanted squeak in your car? I just hate that!

Well, Squeak has lived out the old adage that "the squeaky wheel gets the grease" in positive and negative ways, too. He gets "love grease" from Matt's mom, whom he adores. And he gets a rise out of Matt—because he often responds to Matt's overtures with scratching and biting, for whatever reason. But there is one part of his life where this squeaky cat has not managed to prevail. He's been blocked from "getting the grease" when it comes to going down the local manhole.

There is a manhole just outside Matt's house. Squeak will sit on its iron cover till two or three o'clock in the morning. It's as if he is waiting to pounce on whatever lies beneath. The cover is heavy and strong and fits snugly over this passageway to the underground structure that lies below. But if he could get in, one can only imagine what mischief he would do!

Now, I wouldn't want to compare Squeak with the enemy of our souls. But this cat's behavior does make me think. It makes me realize that Satan is waiting and watching to dive down my "manhole" to the inner workings of my heart and mind. If I don't have my "manhole cover" on tight, he'll slip in and make trouble. One of my more vulnerable times is in the wee hours of the morning.

Sometime in the middle of the night, I usually wake up to heed nature's call. This is when Satan loves to pounce on me. He makes me think of all the countless things I need to do. I lay there in bed, drowning in worry and stress about bills to pay and rooms to clean and stories to write. Then I start to feel ill. Why? Because I let my "manhole cover" slip.

In Ephesians 6:10-11, Paul writes, "Finally, be strong in the Lord and in his mighty power. Put on the full armor of God, so that you can take your stand against the devil's schemes."

My spiritual armor is stronger than any iron manhole cover. It will keep the enemy out, but I have to put it on. I grab my shield of faith and pray. I ask the Father to come between me and the devil. In a whisper, so as not to wake my husband, Steve, I command Satan, "In the name of Jesus, leave and take your helpers with you!" He has no choice but to do so, because God is greater. I imagine myself crawling up into God's lap like a little girl and sleeping sweetly. I can be free of worry and get the rest I need, because my manhole cover is securely back in place.

God's armor also worked for Jesus, when Satan tried to pounce on Him at a time when He was especially vulnerable. Jesus had just spent 40 days in the wilderness. Satan tried three times to tempt Him and turn Him aside from the Father's purpose. Each time Jesus fought back with another piece of God's armor—Scripture. Jesus' manhole cover was firmly in place, and Satan couldn't get in. Finally the enemy left, and angels came and took care of Him.

Squeak is not the enemy, even though he causes Matt grief. But the image of him perched on the manhole is a great reminder that Satan lurks near. He would love to get the "grease" of giving us grief, but we don't have to let him. We can put on our armor and call on God to give our squeaky enemy the boot instead!

Above all else, guard your heart, for everything you do flows from it (Proverbs 4:23).

Consider This:

Under what conditions are you most vulnerable to Satan's attack? What happens when he slips in through your "manhole?" How might putting on God's armor (Ephesians 6:10-18) give him the boot and keep him out in the future?

All Quiet on the Snowy Front
How's Your Spiritual Hearing?

*What matters deafness of the ear, when
the mind hears? The one true deafness, the
incurable deafness, is that of the mind.*

VICTOR HUGO

I usually saw Snowy in our garage or hanging out by our front porch. She was a large, beautiful white cat with blue eyes that paled the sky on a sunny day. Snowy was one of the many cats that shared our country neighborhood, but life was a little different for her, because she was deaf.

If you watched her, you could see how Snowy compensated for her lack of hearing with her other senses. She kept her eyes wide open as she walked, turning her head to look both ways. She seemed to have a keen sense of touch as well.

Snowy learned early on to stay away from the roads. She kept to herself most of the time as she walked around, seeming confident and enjoying herself in her own quiet world. One day I followed her around the garage as she serenely explored the fishing gear, the patio furniture, and other places where she might enjoy taking a nap. Snowy was oblivious to me. Suddenly, she looked up and saw me. She was so startled she leaped in the air and her thick white fur seemed to jump straight up from her skin as she ran off in fright.

Though she was comfortable in her own quiet world, Snowy seemed less at ease when the real world intruded. Normally when another cat or dog or person approached her, she was quick to move away. Sometimes deafness brought other hazards, too. There was a time in her kitten life when she fell asleep behind the rear wheel of a neighbor family's car. As the driver got behind the wheel, someone looking out the kitchen window saw what was about to happen—and screamed. Snowy didn't hear, of course. Neither did the driver. But Snowy must have felt the vibration when the car's engine started, because she quickly moved away. Thanks to her heightened senses the disaster was averted.

After many meetings around my home, Snowy and I became friends. She would join me on the front porch without fear. I would read a book and she would sleep, or both of us would sit together, enjoying the peaceful view. All the while, my dogs Stuart and Squitchey would be barking away in the house, desperate to come out and protect me from this intruder. Snowy sat calm and unruffled, literally deaf to the possible danger. I would of course have protected her, but it was one more reminder of how Snowy's inability to hear put her at risk.

Snowy's situation got me thinking. Though deafness put her at extra risk, she could partially compensate with her other senses. But what happens if we are spiritually deaf? How does dulled hearing to God and His warnings put us at heightened risk in our lives, and what might remedy that?

I once knew someone whose spiritual hearing got dulled. She knew the Lord, but she wasn't strong in her faith. She saw the effect Jesus had on her friends, but she just couldn't seem to grasp it. She said it all sounded too easy. Then she saw a film that shook whatever faith she had. She decided not to believe in God or Jesus at all. She became deaf to anyone who tried to help her understand. This went on for several years. Her friends gave up trying to talk her out of it, but they kept right on praying for her. Maybe she wasn't hearing their words, but God would hear their prayers.

Then one day a young college student came to this woman for help. For whatever reason, she suggested they look for answers in the Bible.

As they were searching, she read the story in Judges 2 about how the Israelites turned from following God to worshiping idols. She saw the trouble it caused them, and realized her own mistake in giving up her belief in her Creator. Her spiritual hearing began to be restored.

Snowy stays alert as best she can, but she needs those around her to watch out for her too. So did the woman whose faith faltered. Her friends' prayers surely played a part in the restoration of her spiritual hearing. So did God's Word, because as Paul writes, "Faith comes from hearing the message, and the message is heard through the word about Christ" (Romans 10:17).

We can all tune up our spiritual hearing through prayer and Bible study and keep listening for the still small voice of God's Holy Spirit. He is faithful to watch over us, but we must stay watchful too, so we "hear" and respond to the warnings He gives.

But the seed on good soil stands for those with a noble and good heart, who hear the word, retain it, and by persevering produce a crop (Luke 8:15).

Consider This:

Have you ever become spiritually hard of hearing? What do you think caused it? What were the results? What restored you? Is there someone in your life whose spiritual hearing you might need to pray for?

You Don't Need a Fleece to See the Fleas

Watch for Signs of Trouble

The bird alighteth not on the spread net when
it beholds another bird in the snare. Take
warning by the misfortunes of others, that
others may not take example from you.

JOHANN WOLFGANG VON GOETHE

It was another gray morning in Los Angeles. Everyone wanted summer to start, but a phenomenon called June Gloom was getting in the way. Some days we don't even see the sun until three or four o'clock in the afternoon, and it's chilly enough to wear a sweater. Even cats are aware of June Gloom and sleep away most of their day. They are also unhappy because of the fleas. Whether it's the dark weather or just the season, fleas seem to multiply at this time of year, so I have to be watchful.

When Midnight awoke from her slumber yesterday, she stretched and then began to lick herself frantically. Later she came in to find my lap, and as I petted her neck I felt bump after bump—fleas. Today I watched her come inside to look for her afternoon snack. She walked slowly across the floor and then suddenly leaped straight into the air.

Then she took a step or two more, leaped again, and finally jumped up onto the counter. I had to feed her there because she wouldn't stay on the floor. After her snack, she jumped down and beelined toward the door. She had almost reached it when she leaped straight up once more. This was my signal to act. I put flea treatment medicine on her. Then I vacuumed all the rooms. Finally, I called our exterminator to spray our yard as soon as possible. In a couple of days, Midnight will be able to walk without leaping because the flea population will be gone. It is vital that I watch for and heed the warning signs of her distress, because if the flea infestation isn't dealt with it can make her sick.

My daughter Sarah must also watch for warning signs to protect a loved one. Her son Jayden has childhood asthma. She goes on alert as soon as he gets a runny nose. She monitors his temperature, watches him closely if he coughs, and listens for shallow, rapid breathing. As soon as she hears a certain kind of cough or notes rapid breathing, she brings out a special machine that helps his lungs to breathe more easily. She knows Jayden's asthma can make him very sick if left untreated—and even culminate in a trip to the emergency room. But she can often ward off the trouble by heeding the signals, just as I do with Midnight and the fleas.

As believers, we also need to stay alert for signs of spiritual ills or "infestations." If we don't know the warning signals, we can get spiritually sick. This is what happened to Julia, a relatively new believer who thought she could combine her Christian faith with worldly attitudes and behavior.

Julia had a group of friends who didn't share her faith in the Lord. They had set aside Thursday afternoons to get together. They would go out to a movie or spend time with each other at one of their homes or at a coffee shop. This in itself was not a bad thing. But instead of being a godly influence on her friends, Julia let their worldly ways infest her life.

Julia didn't notice at first that she behaved differently when she was with these friends. Later she realized she stopped talking about her faith because she wanted them to like her, and she was afraid it would make her seem "different." She went along with their worldly talk, even if it violated biblical principles. If there was something offensive in a movie, she kept silent.

Soon, this infestation of the world began affecting Julia in other ways. She started skipping her time with the Lord. She found herself making excuses not to pray or read the Bible. She still went to church each week, but the songs didn't resonate, and neither did the sermon. Her body was there, but her spirit wasn't.

After a time, one of her church friends recognized warning signals in her life and asked Julia what was up. Julia realized she was "sick" with the world. She prayed and asked God to help her. She opened her Bible and read James 4:4, "Don't you know that friendship with the world means enmity against God?" She said it was as if God Himself spoke those words to her. Julia asked God's forgiveness and help. Soon her passion for the Lord and Scripture returned. She said it taught her a great lesson to watch for the signs of her love growing cold. She also realized she could be a positive witness to her friends by staying true to her faith when she was with them.

Josiah was a godly king of Judah who also saw and heeded spiritual warning signs (2 Kings 22-23). He began ruling as an eight-year-old child. When he was in his twenties, he took steps to have the temple repaired. In the process, the high priest found the Book of the Law. Josiah read it and saw huge warning signals of the people's sin, and God's impending judgment. His kingdom had become infested with the spiritual "fleas" of idolatry. He tore his robes in distress and grief. Josiah could not prevent God's judgment altogether, but because of his humility and repentance, God delayed it till after Josiah's death so he would be spared from seeing the devastation.

Whether it's fleas, or asthma, or an infestation of worldliness, if we watch for and heed warning signs, we'll avoid worse trouble. We must remember that though we are in the world, we must not be "of the world"—because we belong to the Lord.

Do not love the world or anything in the world. If any-
one loves the world, love for the Father is not in him.
For everything in the world—the lust of the flesh, the

lust of the eyes, and the pride of life—comes not from the Father but from the world. The world and its desires pass away, but whoever does the will of God lives forever (1 John 2:15-17).

Consider This:

What signals can you watch for to warn you that you are getting caught up in the world? How can you rectify the situation? Do you have friends that can help you spot danger signs? How can you be that kind of friend to others?

The Cat That Faxed
Beware Who You "Dial"

*One part of knowledge consists in
being ignorant of such things as
are not worthy to be known.*

SOCRATES

Perry is a beautiful orange cat that lives with my in-laws, Harold and Doris. They let him sleep pretty much wherever he wants to. He has his choice of many soft, comfortable places. There is a nice comfy sofa in the den where the light is perfect in the morning. He can also curl up on some lounging chairs in the same room. He loves to sleep on the back of Harold's recliner when Harold is sitting there. And at night he gets to sleep with Harold and Doris in their big king-size bed.

But there was one spot Perry chose that turned out to be a problem. In the afternoon, Perry liked to lay his big, fluffy body right on top of the office fax machine. Doris wasn't concerned at first. But one day, she realized that Perry had actually called someone on the phone. She was in the other room and heard someone yelling hello and asking if anyone was there. When she walked into the office, she saw Perry jump off the fax machine. Once he did so, the voice got much clearer. Doris realized her cat had accidentally "called" a stranger. She picked up the receiver and tried to explain what happened, but the story was just too unbelievable to comprehend. Doris finally apologized and hung up. After that, Doris moved the fax machine to a spot that Perry wouldn't be able to access. She was helping him stay out of trouble by keeping him out of the wrong place so he couldn't "call" the wrong people.

Thinking of Perry sitting on the fax machine calling strangers makes us laugh. But it didn't put Perry at risk. It was a problem for his owners and the people he phoned, but not for him. Since he's a cat and doesn't speak English, he couldn't understand anything that was said by the people he mistakenly "dialed." But his escapade made me realize that if we humans wind up in the wrong place and dial the wrong people, the results may be much more concerning.

Just this afternoon I was in the wrong place dialing up the "wrong number" on my television set. I was listening to a show that was giving life advice. They were talking about seeking a god within us to help, rather than praying to the God of the Bible. I should have run from this "wrong number," but I didn't. Fortunately, my husband, Steve, walked in. He knew I was supposed to be writing—working on stories for this book. He gently asked what I was watching and whether I felt okay. His gracious questions prodded me to "hang up" on that wrong number and seek truth in my Bible instead.

Looking back, I realize I was doing a Perry thing. I was sitting on the wrong "facts machine," dialing the wrong number, and listening to something that had nothing to do with my life. I'm so glad that God is my Lord and Savior and Guide and I can find life answers in His Word. And I'm grateful that my husband and best friend Steve helped me disconnect from that wrong number, just as Doris did with Perry.

Choosing the wrong information circuit is a common human problem. We don't have to go very far in the Bible to read about it. Way back in the Garden of Eden, the very first woman, Eve, listened to the serpent when he urged her to disobey God. God had commanded, "You are free to eat from any tree in the garden; but you must not eat from the tree of the knowledge of good and evil, for when you eat from it you will certainly die" (Genesis 2:16-17). But the serpent told her they wouldn't die—they would become like God. Eve not only listened to the serpent and acted on this lie; she got Adam to eat the forbidden fruit too. Sin and death entered the world from that point and all humanity and creation are still suffering the repercussions today.

Perry needed Doris' help not to "call" the wrong number. I needed Steve's help to step away from the wrong "facts machine." We all need God to show us the difference between His truth and Satan's lies. But if we seek to follow Him and ask for His wisdom, He will delight to guide us on His path.

*Show me your ways, L*ORD*, teach me your paths. Guide me in your truth and teach me, for you are God my Savior, and my hope is in you all day long (Psalm 25:4-5).*

Consider This:

Have you ever sat on the wrong "facts machine"? What misinformation did you get? Did you act on it or were you redirected? What was the result? Do you know someone who's being misled that you might gently redirect to seek God?

Once an Alley Cat...
We Need God to Break Strongholds

Habit is either the best of servants
or the worst of masters.

Nathaniel Emmons

Gabriel was living proof that you can take the cat out of the alley, but you can't always take the alley out of the cat. Maybe that was at least partly my fault. I introduced him to the alley in the first place.

I got Gabe as a very young kitten—about six weeks of age. He was a beautiful longhaired black and white "all American" mixed breed. In those days I lived in a town house, and I didn't want a litter box inside—so my cats were indoor-outdoor. When Gabe was old enough I let him use the cat door. He loved going in and out at will and roaming the alley on my suburban Los Angeles block.

Being an alley cat suited Gabe, but there came a time when a neighbor objected. Gabe was spraying on his doorstep. I spent a month struggling to keep my cat in. I blocked his access to the cat door. Gabe proceeded to try to slip past me every time I used my human door. Finally I got tired of fighting and let him go out again. I hoped against hope that he'd stop spraying so the neighbor wouldn't mind.

Somehow things worked out with the neighbor. But I found new drawbacks to Gabe being an alley cat. I couldn't always get him in when I wanted to. At one point, he'd vanish for a day or more at a time. Finally, I spied him perched in someone else's window. Like many cats, he'd adopted a new person. She hadn't been sure what his situation was. I asked her not to let him in, and she complied. But he was still a roamer, and at times I'd be out in that alley at midnight, searching for my wayward truant to bring him home.

Gabe was an alley cat till he was about nine years old. Then one day he trotted through the cat door...and vanished. I searched and searched, but I never found him. Maybe he was scooped up, or ran off, or got hit by a car. To this day I don't know what became of my black and white buddy. All the cats I've had since Gabe haven't been allowed outside. Letting a cat out caused too much angst. Maybe I couldn't switch Gabe's behavior—but he switched mine!

Cats are not the only ones whose behavior patterns are hard to change. I have had habits so stubborn they've turned into strongholds. Some of my greatest behavioral struggles have involved weight and food.

My weight problems started in fourth or fifth grade. I had a slightly slow metabolism, but I also ate for comfort. I got chunky. Other kids teased me. Mom and Dad wanted me to slim down for health reasons. I rebelled—but finally, in high school, I decided to go on a diet. I went too far, and like many young girls, became anorexic. Dad stepped in, took charge, and solved the immediate crisis. But like Gabe, though he took the cat out of the alley, he didn't take the alley out of the cat. As one therapist put it years later, I was still anorexic in my head. I binged. I ate compulsively late at night. I dieted off and on. I weighed myself obsessively—several times a day. And I let my weight control my mood and emotions way too much.

My struggles with weight and food did serve one useful purpose. They fueled the search I was already on to find God. They made me miserable and showed me my need. There were many other factors too, but the sense that there had to be something more to life than this certainly helped prepare me to ask Jesus into my heart in my junior year of college.

I wish I could say that finding God ended my weight obsession. The truth is, it has been a lifelong struggle. Like the Egyptians of Joseph's day, I've had fat years and lean years. I've had on-and-off struggles with compulsive eating and compulsive weighing. This whole area is a stronghold, and an idol, in my life.

It's not always easy to be transparent as a person or a writer. I want to write that my food hang-ups have been conquered. They haven't. My old devils don't want to go quietly into the sunset.

I have cried on a dear friend's shoulder about how old bugbears (my own and others') just don't seem to stay "fixed." She has reminded me that this life is messy. Our spiritual enemy, Satan, knows our weaknesses and keeps hammering at them…and we can't live holy lives or conquer our strongholds in our own strength.

If it's any consolation (and at times it isn't), we're in rather good company on this one. No less a personage than the apostle Paul faced such struggles. His flesh kept on fighting his new nature and he didn't like it. In Romans 7:18-19 he wrote, "For I have the desire to do what is good, but I cannot carry it out. For I do not do the good I want to do, but the evil I do not want to do—this I keep on doing." Paul had hope, though. In verses 24-25 of this same chapter, he added, "What a wretched man I am! Who will rescue me from this body that is subject to death? Thanks be to God, who delivers me through Jesus Christ our Lord!"

Unlike Gabe, all God's children can know that we won't be "alley cats" forever! One day, we will leave this life and enter God's presence. When we do, we will be saved not only from the penalty of sin, but from its presence also. Meanwhile, as we surrender more and more of ourselves to our Lord, He is at work in us, breaking down what is holding us back so we can be forever free in Him!

For it is God who works in you to will and to act in order to fulfill his good purpose (Philippians 2:13).

Consider This:

Do you have persistent habits or behaviors that are enslaving you? Have you tried to conquer them in your own strength? What was the result? Do you believe God wants to free you from these strongholds? Will you pray and ask Him to do so? What Scriptures might encourage you?

Howl, Moochie, Howl

Guard Your Spiritual Territory

*The closer we walk to the Shepherd, the
farther we are from the wolf.*

ANONYMOUS

One night I was sleeping soundly when suddenly my peace was shattered by a loud, screeching howl. I leaped out of bed, raced downstairs, and opened the side door. Mooch wasn't there, so I crept out the front door in my PJs and began searching for my male cat under the cars in the driveway. "Moochie, Moochie, where are you?" I whispered. Just then I heard a huge thump on the gate as Mooch and an unidentified feline intruder shrieked at each other. Judging by the noise, I thought Mooch might come in a bit bloodied by the encounter. He proved me wrong a couple of minutes later. Mooch pranced in like a victorious warrior, tail and head held high as he trotted happily over to me. He had no observable problems whatsoever and he seemed so proud of himself that I petted him and told him, "Good boy!" After all, he had been protecting his territory from the enemy!

Male cats are especially territorial and will fight to guard what they perceive as their jurisdiction. When we adopted him, Mooch came to us with two small chunks out of his ears as a result of his former battles, and now he was willing to add more scars.

As I went back upstairs to bed, I thought about my human kids, now grown. Two have children of their own, and they must protect them from the potential "enemies" of this life. My daughter Sarah has two little boys under the age of three. Eli, her younger son, loves trash cans so much that he has added the words *black, blue,* and *green,* as well as *full* and *empty,* to his 18-month-old vocabulary. When he's out front and spies a trash can, he makes a mad dash to see it "up close and personal." But Sarah and her husband Dan are careful to guard Eli from the potential dangers of the street, so they are teaching him to stay on the sidewalk regardless of where his beloved trash cans are placed. They are diligent about protecting Eli from what could harm him.

My older son Sam and his wife Andrea are also diligent about protecting their three children—and for them this involves not just physical safety, but guarding their hearts and minds. Owen, their eight-year-old, is at an age where he goes to movies with friends. Sam and Andrea do their research before saying "yes" to a film. Afterwards, they discuss it with him to see what it might be saying about God. Sam and Andrea are helping to develop critical thinking in Owen so he can stand firm in his faith.

I know that Sarah, like Sam, will guard her boys spiritually as they get older. I had no such training growing up. I wasn't brought up in any faith, although I had good parents who gave me a loving and moral environment. Somehow this void made me more intrigued with the spiritual realm. But because I didn't know how to guard this area of my life, I became entangled with the enemy by using astrology and a Ouija board. This resulted in some scary demonic encounters. When I first received Jesus, I was instructed to get rid of all the paraphernalia that had occultist ties, and to renounce them out loud.

I obeyed. But the evil beings didn't go "quietly into the night." I quickly had to learn how to fight for my new territory. My fighting wasn't like Mooch's, since the battle was in my mind. I had to learn to stand up to the evil beings in the name of Jesus, demanding that they leave. And leave they did, because I belonged to Him and had the authority to use His powerful Name. I was learning to do what Paul urges in Ephesians 6:10-18, to guard my spiritual territory by standing firm in Christ and putting on "the full armor of God."

Elisha, a prophet of Israel in Old Testament days, understood this battle. One morning his servant awoke to find vast enemy forces surrounding the city where they were. "'Oh no, my lord! What shall we do?' the servant asked. 'Don't be afraid,' the prophet answered. 'Those who are with us are more than those who are with them.' And Elisha prayed, 'Open his eyes, LORD, so that he may see.' Then the LORD opened the servant's eyes, and he looked and saw the hills full of horses and chariots of fire all around Elisha" (2 Kings 6:15-17).

Elisha's servant was now able to see the even greater spiritual forces there to protect them. The battle was already won, because God's army was on their side. It's the same with our battles. Jesus has conquered the enemy, so it's His power that wins each battle we fight.

We can win our spiritual battles, but we must guard our spiritual territory by putting on God's full armor. Then we can be like Mooch and protect our turf!

The weapons we fight with are not the weapons of the world. On the contrary, they have divine power to demolish strongholds (2 Corinthians 10:4).

Consider This:

What are the greatest spiritual battles you face right now? What "enemy tactics" cause you the most trouble? What spiritual weapons might help you protect your territory? Which might help you do battle for others who might be in danger?

Everett's Watch Cat

God Is Our Protector

*Don't think there are no crocodiles
because the water is calm.*

MALAYAN PROVERB

Maya is a very special Bengal cat that belongs to my niece Kim and her husband, Jeff. They chose her out of her litter because she was the sweet one curled up in the corner. Two weeks later, what do you know? A tiny growl came out of their shy little bundle. They loved it!

These days, Maya's growl is deep and throaty. She growls when you pet her or bring her in from outside. She wants to be in your presence, but she's not big on cuddling. No need to touch her unless she invites you. She is also oh, so cautious. She literally walks around the house low to the ground. She always seems to be on the prowl, and it's quite fun to watch.

There is, however, one human who gets special treatment from Maya—Kim's little son Everett. When Everett was born, Maya changed. She became more tender. And she seemed to appoint herself Everett's "watch cat." She wants to be with him all the time.

Maya is also more tolerant with Everett. She can get a little scary when you get her angry. Petting her too much will do that. But with Everett, she acts a bit differently. If he pets her once she doesn't mind.

With the next pet, she growls a little warning Everett hasn't caught onto yet. The third time, she makes a statement but never hurts him. She just lets out a deep growl and moves ever so slowly away from him. But it takes almost no time before she is right back by his side.

My husband, Steve, is my "watch cat." He has helped to save my life on more than one occasion. A few years ago, we were having lunch in our home when I started feeling ill. I told him I was experiencing some pain around my heart and I had heartburn. I didn't think I needed instant attention, but he insisted we go to the doctor right away. It turns out if he hadn't taken me, I probably would have died. I ended up having a quadruple heart bypass. Steve stayed by my side, called the family, and prayed me through. He was my protector and "watch cat" through one of the scariest times of my life.

Maya and Steve are faithful to watch over those they love, but there's only so much they can do. If something threatened Everett, Maya could sound an alarm, but she probably couldn't save his life. Steve couldn't fix my heart, though he got me help. Even the doctors who performed my bypass surgery didn't have ultimate power over life and death. God does. He is my ultimate Protector. He held my life in His hands that day, and always will.

Many centuries ago, God also held Ruth's life in His hands. This Moabite widow left her homeland and family to go to Israel with her mother-in-law Naomi. It was harvest time. Ruth went to glean leftover grain, as was permitted, so they would have food. God led her to the field of Naomi's close relative, Boaz. When Boaz learned that she had left her family and stayed with the mother of her dead husband, his heart was moved. He commanded that she be guarded and given favor in his fields. He was her "watch cat."

Before long, Boaz became an even greater protector. According to Jewish law, if a woman was widowed, male relatives could function as "kinsman redeemers." They could acquire the dead man's property and marry his widow to perpetuate his family name. At Naomi's direction, Ruth asked Boaz to do this for her—and he did. In time, Ruth bore Boaz a child—King David's grandfather. And many centuries later, Ruth's line would produce the greatest Kinsman Redeemer and Protector of all—our Messiah, God's Son, Jesus.

Boaz was faithful to watch over the one he loved. Maya and Steve are too. It's wonderful to have someone who cares for you in this way. But cats and humans are limited in their ability to care for us. God isn't. He knows and sees everything, is everywhere, and promises never to leave or forsake us. We can only imagine what God has in store for us if we put our trust in Him!

You are my hiding place; you will protect me from trouble and surround me with songs of deliverance (Psalm 32:7).

Consider This:

Has someone ever been your "watch cat"? Did they ever save you from trouble? How did they bless your life? Have you ever been someone's "watch cat"? What did you do and how did it help? How has God's watchful care protected you and those you love?

CAT TAILS...ER, TALES...BY AUTHOR

DOTTIE P. ADAMS

Meet the Authors

M.R. Wells has written extensively for children's animated television and video programming, including several Disney shows, the animated PBS series *Adventures from The Book of Virtues*, and the action video series *Bibleman*. She has co-written three other devotional books for pet lovers. She shares her Southern California home with the kitties and puppies she adores: Muffin, Bo, Munchie, Becca, and Marley.

Connie Fleishauer is a teacher and writer and enjoys filmmaking. She is also trained in voice-over work. This is her fourth pet lovers' devotional. She is the wife of a California farmer, a mother of three, a mother-in-law of two, and a grandma of one. She was friend and co-master to Kitty and many other cats that warmed the Fleishauer's home. Currently she and her husband care for Stuart, a Welsh Corgi, and Squitchey, a little rescued dog.

Dottie P. Adams is a Teaching Director for Community Bible Study and has taught a Los Angeles-area Bible class for 20 years. With her current coauthors, she wrote *Purr-ables from Heaven: Devotions for Cat Lovers*. She's the wife of a retired physicist whom she adores. She's also the mother of three grown children and grandma to five. An ardent photographer, she creates annual photo/journal albums of her family. Dottie has loved cats from childhood and is grateful to God for creating purring creatures that are so beautiful, funny, and endearing, especially Midnight and Mooch.

Visit the authors' website at www.fourpawsfromheaven.com

Purr-ables from Heaven

Cats are quirky, but we adore them anyway—perhaps because they're a lot like us. This delightful book of devotions illustrates how even the most contradictory creatures can thrive in the presence of a loving, ever-patient owner. Each humorous and encouraging tale inspires us to delight in the Lord and lap up His loving presence.

Four Paws from Heaven

Animal lovers will celebrate this pack of short dog tales and human stories. The enjoyable devotions provide entertaining and valuable lessons of faith, loyalty, and joy gleaned while walking through life alongside four paws.

Paws for Reflection

More than 50 humorous, poignant, and spiritually insightful stories are packed together under themed sections, including *Paws for Love: Curl Up with the Master*. This gathering of short devotions reveals the faithfulness and companionship we get from canines and shares related insights for getting the most out of life.

Four Paws from Heaven Gift Edition

Three gifted writers and one internationally acclaimed animal photographer combine their talents in this heartwarming, encouraging collection of short stories and inspirational lessons every dog lover should own. Rachael Hale's photographs capture the true heart and nature of man's beloved best friend. Authors Wells, Young, and Fleishauer delight readers with their very own true-to-life, tail-wagging pet stories, reflections on God's loving-kindness, and encouragement to live each day obedient to the call of faith.

Pet lovers will jump at the chance to learn from their furry, four-pawed friends! They'll yip about the amazing photos and yap about them with their friends. Best of all, they will be inspired to stay loyal to the Master. Truly a dog lover's companion, this gift book is sure to fetch a smile.

Purr-ables from Heaven Gift Edition

Cat lovers will absolutely purr over Rachael Hale's photographs of playful kittens, cats of all colors, and fancy felines. Page after page, charming and amusing photos invite the reader into a world of furry fun. Authors Wells, Fleishauer, and Adams take turns sharing their own cat tales, encouraging readers to look at life through the bright eyes of their pets. Skillfully woven into the heart of each sweet story is a gentle reminder of God's love and faithfulness.

Every cat lover will be inspired to curl up with this cozy little story collection and appreciate their feline friend even more. It's all about cats—soft and warm, cuddly and cute, sometimes finicky but definitely fun!

To learn more about books by M.R. Wells,
Dottie P. Adams, and Connie Fleishauer, or to read
sample chapters, log on to our website:

www.harvesthousepublishers.com

HARVEST HOUSE PUBLISHERS

EUGENE, OREGON